TRIBE

ALSO BY SEBASTIAN JUNGER

The Perfect Storm

Fire

A Death in Belmont

War

TRIBE

On Homecoming and Belonging

SEBASTIAN JUNGER

4th ESTATE • *London*

4th Estate
An imprint of HarperCollins*Publishers*
1 London Bridge Street
London SE1 9GF
www.4thEstate.co.uk

This edition first published in Great Britain in 2016 by 4th Estate

First published in the United States in 2016 by Twelve,
an imprint of Grand Central Publishing

A catalogue record for this book is
available from the British Library

ISBN (HB) 978-0-00-816817-9
ISBN (TPB) 978-0-00-816821-6

Certain short sections of the article "How PTSD Became a Problem Far
Beyond the Battlefield" from the June 2015 issue of *Vanity Fair* magazine
appear virtually unaltered in this book

Printed and bound in Great Britain by
Clays Ltd, St Ives plc

This book is dedicated to my brothers,
John, Emery, and Chief

CONTENTS

AUTHOR'S NOTE

This book grew out of an article that I wrote for the June 2015 issue of *Vanity Fair* titled "How PTSD Became a Problem Far Beyond the Battlefield." Certain short sections of that article appear virtually unaltered in this book.

I have included all source material for this book in a section titled "Source Notes." I do not use footnotes because this is not an academic book and footnotes can interfere with the ease of reading. Nevertheless, I felt that certain scientific studies about modern society, about combat, and about post-traumatic stress disorder had the potential to greatly surprise or even upset some readers. With that in mind, I decided to include at least a cursory mention of the source within the text so that in certain cases, readers could quickly verify the information for themselves.

Both the book and the article include phrases that some people find problematic or even offensive. The first is "American Indian." Many people prefer the term "Native American," although when I tried to use that with an Apache interview subject named Gregory Gomez, he pointed out that the term properly refers to people of any ethnicity born in the United States. He insisted that I use "American Indian" instead, and so I have.

The other problematic phrase is "post-traumatic stress disorder." Some people understandably feel that the word "disorder" risks stigmatizing those who continue to struggle with wartime trauma. I ultimately decided to retain the word because any long-term traumatic reactions would seem to qualify as a "disruption of normal physical or mental functions," as the *Oxford American Dictionary* defines the word "disorder." Most health care workers—and many soldiers—agreed with that position.

Finally, this book includes several first-person accounts of events that happened many years ago, in some cases before I was even a journalist. Those scenes are retrieved from my memory without the benefit of notes, and the dialogue was not recorded in any way except by my memory. Ordinarily, speech enclosed by quotation marks should be documented with a tape recorder or notebook, and any event should be written down as it happened or shortly thereafter. In the case of these few stories, however, I had to rely entirely on my memory. After giving the matter much thought, I decided that doing so was within my journalistic standards as long as I was clear with my readers about my lack of documentation. The people in those stories have been in my mind my entire life and have often served as crucial moral guides to my own behavior. I only wish I knew who all of them were so that I could thank them somehow.

INTRODUCTION

In the fall of 1986, just out of college, I set out to
hitchhike across the northwestern part of the United
States. I'd hardly ever been west of the Hudson River,
and in my mind what waited for me out in Dakota
and Wyoming and Montana was not only the real
America but the real me as well. I'd grown up in a
Boston suburb where people's homes were set behind
deep hedges or protected by huge yards and neighbors hardly knew each other. And they didn't need
to: nothing ever happened in my town that required
anything close to a collective effort. Anything bad
that happened was taken care of by the police or the
fire department, or at the very least the town main-
tenance crews. (I worked for them one summer. I
remember shoveling a little too hard one day and the

foreman telling me to slow down because, as he said, "Some of us have to get through a lifetime of this.")

The sheer predictability of life in an American suburb left me hoping—somewhat irresponsibly—for a hurricane or a tornado or *something* that would require us to all band together to survive. Something that would make us feel like a tribe. What I wanted wasn't destruction and mayhem but the opposite: solidarity. I wanted the chance to prove my worth to my community and my peers, but I lived in a time and a place where nothing dangerous ever really happened. Surely this was new in the human experience, I thought. How do you become an adult in a society that doesn't ask for sacrifice? How do you become a man in a world that doesn't require courage?

Those kinds of tests clearly weren't going to happen in my hometown, but putting myself in a situation where I had very little control—like hitchhiking across the country—seemed like a decent substitute. That's how I wound up outside Gillette, Wyoming, one morning in late October 1986, with my pack leaned against the guardrail and an interstate map in my back pocket. Semis rattled over the bridge spacers and hurtled on toward the Rockies a hundred miles away. Pickup trucks passed with men in them who turned to stare as they went by. A few unrolled their window and threw beer bottles at me that exploded harmlessly against the asphalt.

In my pack I had a tent and sleeping bag, a set of aluminum cookpots, and a Swedish-made camping stove that ran on gasoline and had to be pressurized with a thumb pump. That and a week's worth of food was all I had with me outside Gillette, Wyoming, that morning, when I saw a man walking toward me up the on-ramp from town.

From a distance I could see that he wore a quilted old canvas union suit and carried a black lunch box. I took my hands out of my pockets and turned to face him. He walked up and stood there studying me. His hair was wild and matted and his union suit was shiny with filth and grease at the thighs. He didn't look unkindly but I was young and alone and I watched him like a hawk. He asked me where I was headed.

"California," I said. He nodded.

"How much food do you got?" he asked.

I thought about this. I had plenty of food—along with all the rest of my gear—and he obviously didn't have much. I'd give food to anyone who said he was hungry, but I didn't want to get robbed, and that's what seemed was about to happen.

"Oh, I just got a little cheese," I lied. I stood there, ready, but he just shook his head.

"You can't get to California on just a little cheese," he said. "You need more than that."

The man said that he lived in a broken-down car and that every morning he walked three miles to a coal mine outside of town to see if they needed fill-in work. Some days they did, some days they didn't, and this was one of the days that they didn't. "So I won't be needing this," he said, opening his black lunch box. "I saw you from town and just wanted to make sure you were okay."

The lunch box contained a bologna sandwich, an apple, and a bag of potato chips. The food had probably come from a local church. I had no choice but to take it. I thanked him and put the food in my pack for later and wished him luck. Then he turned and made his way back down the on-ramp toward Gillette.

I thought about that man for the rest of my trip. I thought about him for the rest of my life. He'd been generous, yes, but lots of people are generous; what made him different was the fact that he'd taken *responsibility* for me. He'd spotted me from town and walked half a mile out a highway to make sure I was okay. Robert Frost famously wrote that home is the place where, when you have to go there, they have to take you in. The word "tribe" is far harder to define, but a start might be the people you feel compelled to share the last of your food with. For reasons I'll never know, the man in Gillette decided to treat me like a member of his tribe.

This book is about why that sentiment is such a rare and precious thing in modern society, and how the lack of it has affected us all. It's about what we can learn from tribal societies about loyalty and belonging and the eternal human quest for meaning. It's about why—for many people—war feels better than peace and hardship can turn out to be a great blessing and disasters are sometimes remembered more fondly than weddings or tropical vacations. Humans don't mind hardship, in fact they thrive on it; what they mind is not feeling necessary. Modern society has perfected the art of making people not feel necessary.

It's time for that to end.

TRIBE

THE MEN AND
THE DOGS

PERHAPS THE SINGLE MOST STARTLING FACT ABOUT
America is that, alone among the modern nations that
have become world powers, it did so while butted up
against three thousand miles of howling wilderness
populated by Stone-Age tribes. From King Philip's
War in the 1600s until the last Apache cattle raids
across the Rio Grande in 1924, America waged an
ongoing campaign against a native population that
had barely changed, technologically, in 15,000 years.
Over the course of three centuries, America became a
booming industrial society that was cleaved by class
divisions and racial injustice but glued together by a
body of law that, theoretically at least, saw all people as equal. The Indians, on the other hand, lived

communally in mobile or semi-permanent encampments that were more or less run by consensus and broadly egalitarian. Individual authority was earned rather than seized and imposed only on people who were willing to accept it. Anyone who didn't like it was free to move somewhere else.

The proximity of these two cultures over the course of many generations presented both sides with a stark choice about how to live. By the end of the nineteenth century, factories were being built in Chicago and slums were taking root in New York while Indians fought with spears and tomahawks a thousand miles away. It may say something about human nature that a surprising number of Americans— mostly men—wound up joining Indian society rather than staying in their own. They emulated Indians, married them, were adopted by them, and on some occasions even fought alongside them. And the opposite almost never happened: Indians almost never ran away to join white society. Emigration always seemed to go from the civilized to the tribal, and it left Western thinkers flummoxed about how to explain such an apparent rejection of their society.

"When an Indian child has been brought up among us, taught our language and habituated to our customs,"

Benjamin Franklin wrote to a friend in 1753, "[yet] if he goes to see his relations and make one Indian ramble with them, there is no persuading him ever to return."

On the other hand, Franklin continued, white captives who were liberated from the Indians were almost impossible to keep at home: "Tho' ransomed by their friends, and treated with all imaginable tenderness to prevail with them to stay among the English, yet in a short time they become disgusted with our manner of life...and take the first good opportunity of escaping again into the woods."

The preference for tribal life among many whites was a problem that played out in particularly wrenching ways during the Pennsylvania frontier wars of the 1760s. In the spring of 1763, an Ottawa Indian leader named Pontiac convened a council of tribes along a small river named the Ecorces, near the former French trading post at Detroit, in what is now the state of Michigan. The steady advance of white settlements was a threat that unified the Indian tribes in ways that no amount of peace and prosperity ever could, and Pontiac thought that with a broad enough alliance, he might push the whites back to where they had been a generation or two earlier. Among the Indians were hundreds of white settlers who had been captured from frontier communities and adopted into the tribes. Some were content with their new families and some were not, but collectively they were of enormous political concern to the colonial authorities.

The meeting of the tribes was coordinated by runners who could cover a hundred miles in a day and who delivered gifts of shell wampum belts and tobacco along with the message of urgent assembly. The belts were beaded in such a way that even distant tribes would understand that the meeting was set for the fifteenth day of *Iskigamizige-Giizis*, the sap-boiling moon. Groups of Indians drifted into Riviere Ecorces and encamped along the banks of the river until finally, on the morning of what English settlers knew as April 27, old men began passing through the camp calling the warriors to council.

"They issued from their cabins: the tall, naked figures of the wild Ojibwas, with quivers slung at their backs, and light war-clubs resting in the hollow of their arms," historian Francis Parkman wrote a century later. "Ottawas, wrapped close in their gaudy blankets; Wyandots, fluttering in painted shirts, their heads adorned with feathers and their leggings garnished with bells. All were soon seated within a wide circle upon the grass, row within row, a grave and silent assembly."

Pontiac was known for his high oratory, and by the end of the day he'd convinced the assembled warriors that the future of their people was at stake. Three hundred warriors marched on the English fort, with 2,000 more fighters waiting in the woods for the signal to attack. After initially trying to take the fort by stealth, they withdrew and attacked naked and screaming, with bullets in their mouths for easy reloading. The attempt failed, but soon afterward, the entire frontier erupted in war. Virtually every out-fort and stockade from the upper Allegheny to the Blue Ridge was assaulted simultaneously. Le Boeuf, Venango, Presque Isle, La Baye, St. Joseph, Miamis, Ouchtanon, Sandusky, and Michilimackinac were overrun and their defenders massacred. Scalping parties fanned out through the woodlands and descended upon remote farms and settlements up and down the eastern escarpment, killing an estimated 2,000 settlers. Survivors fled eastward until the Pennsylvania frontier basically started at Lancaster and Carlisle.

The English response was slow but unstoppable. The remnants of the 42nd and 77th Highlander Infantry, recently returned from military action in Cuba, were mustered at the military barracks in Carlisle and prepared for the 200-mile march to Fort Pitt. They were joined by 700 local militia and 30 backwoods scouts and hunters. The Highlanders were supposed to protect the column's flanks but were taken off the job almost immediately because they kept getting lost in the woods. The commander was a young Swiss colonel named Henri Bouquet who had seen combat in Europe and joined the English to advance his career. His orders were simple: march across Pennsylvania, with axmen clearing the way for his wagons, and reinforce Fort Pitt and other beleaguered garrisons on the frontier. No prisoners were to be taken. Native women and children were to be captured and sold into slavery. And bounties were to be paid for any scalp, male or female, that white settlers managed to carve from an Indian head.

Bouquet's army lumbered out of Carlisle in July 1763 and within months had defeated the Indians at Bushy Run and reinforced Fort Pitt and several outlying garrisons. The following summer they carried their campaign into the heart of Indian territory. Sometimes covering five miles, sometimes covering ten, Bouquet's army ground its way through the rich, flat country of the Ohio River basin. They passed through great stands of hardwood and open savannahs fed by innumerable creeks and rivers. Some of the rivers had gravel beaches running for miles that afforded clear passage for the column's supply wagons. The timber was mostly free of underbrush and could be passed easily by men on foot or on horseback. It was a kind of paradise that they were traveling through, and Bouquet's journals mention the natural beauty of the land on almost every page.

By mid-October, Bouquet had gained Muskegham River, deep in Shawnee and Delaware territory, and an Indian delegation met with him to sue for peace. Hoping to intimidate them, Bouquet deployed his forces across an adjacent meadow: rank upon rank of men-at-arms with their bayonets fixed; kilted Highlanders arrayed behind their regimental flags; and dozens of backwoodsmen dressed much like the Indians and leaning confidently on their rifles in a way that must have been enormously reassuring to a European colonel in the wilderness.

First and foremost, Bouquet demanded the immediate return of all white prisoners, and any delay would be considered a declaration of war. During the next few weeks around 200 captives were brought in, more than half of them women and children and many too young to remember having lived otherwise. Some had forgotten their Christian names and were recorded in the ledgers with descriptions such as Redjacket, Bighead, Soremouth, and Sourplums. Dozens of white relatives of the missing had accompanied Bouquet's forces from Fort Pitt, and in addition to the many joyful reunions, there were also wrenching scenes of grief and confusion: young women married to Indian men now standing reluctantly before their former families; children screaming as they were pulled from their Indian kin and delivered to people they didn't recognize and probably considered enemies.

The Indians seemed universally anguished to give up their family members, and when Bouquet's army finally decamped for Fort Pitt in early November, many trailed behind the column, hunting game for their loved ones and trying to delay the final goodbye as long as possible. One Mingo brave refused to leave the side of a young Virginia woman despite warnings that her former family would kill him on sight. "It must not be denied that there were even some grown persons who shewed an unwillingness to return," William Smith, a contemporary of Bouquet's, admitted about some of the white captives.

"The Shawanese were obliged to bind several of their prisoners...and some women, who had been delivered up, afterward found means to escape and run back to the Indian towns."

The reluctance of Bouquet's captives to leave their adopted tribe raised awkward questions about the supposed superiority of Western society. It was understood why young children would not want to return to their original families, and it made sense that renegades like the infamous Simon Girty would later seek refuge with the Indians and even fight alongside them. But as Benjamin Franklin pointed out, there were numerous settlers who were captured as adults and still seemed to prefer Indian society to their own. And what about people who *voluntarily* joined the Indians? What about men who walked off into the tree line and never came home? The frontier was full of men who joined Indian tribes, married Indian women, and lived their lives completely outside civilization.

"Thousands of Europeans are Indians, and we have no examples of even one of those Aborigines having from choice become European," a French émigré named Hector de Crèvecoeur lamented in 1782. "There must be in their social bond something

9

singularly captivating and far superior to anything to be boasted of among us."

Crèvecoeur seemed to have understood that the intensely communal nature of an Indian tribe held an appeal that the material benefits of Western civilization couldn't necessarily compete with. If he was right, that problem started almost as soon as Europeans touched American shores. As early as 1612, Spanish authorities noted in amazement that forty or fifty Virginians had married into Indian tribes, and that even English women were openly mingling with the natives. At that point, whites had been in Virginia for only a few years, and many who joined the Indians would have been born and raised in England. These were not rough frontiersmen who were sneaking off to join the savages; these were the sons and daughters of Europe.

"Notwithstanding the Indian women have all the fuel and bread to procure, and the cooking to perform, their task is probably not harder than that of white women," wrote a Seneca captive named Mary Jemison at the end of her long life. Jemison, who was taken from her family's farm on the Pennsylvania frontier at age fifteen, became so enamored of Seneca life that she once hid from a white search party that had come looking for her. "We had no master to oversee or drive us, so that we could work as leisurely as we pleased," she explained. "No people can live more happy than the Indians did in times of peace . . . Their lives were a continual round of pleasures."

In an attempt to stem the flow of young people into the woods, Virginia and other colonies imposed severe penalties on anyone who took up with the Indians. The Puritan leaders of New England found it particularly galling that anyone would turn their back on Christian society: "People are ready to run wild into the woods again and to be as Heathenish as ever if you do not prevent it," an early Puritan named Increase Mather complained in a tract called *Discourse Concerning the Danger of Apostasy.* Mather was an early administrator of Harvard who spent his life combating—and criminalizing—any relaxation of the Puritan moral code. It was a futile battle. The nature of the frontier was that it kept expanding beyond the reach of church and state, and out on the fringes, people tended to do what they wanted.

The Indian manner was clearly suited to the wilderness, and it wasn't long before frontiersmen began to shed their European clothing and openly emulate people they often referred to as "savages." They dressed in buckskin and open-backed leggings and had muslin breechclouts strapped between their legs. Some even attended Sunday service that way, which so distracted the girls at one church that their minister accused them of not listening to his sermons. The men smoked tobacco and carried tomahawks in their belts and picked up Indian languages and customs. They learned to track and stalk game and move quickly and quietly in the woods, and they adopted what the Puritans dismissed as a "skulking way of war." They fought from concealment as individuals, in other words, rather than lining up like tin soldiers.

"The men and the dogs have a fine time, but the poor women have to suffer," one pioneer wife wrote to her sister about life on the frontier. She complained that her husband—a man named George—refused to make their newborn son a plank cradle, and just gave her a hollowed-out log instead. The boy's only shirt was woven of nettle bark and his pillow was carved out of wood. When his mother pointed out that he was getting sores and rashes, George said that the hardships would just toughen him up for hunting later in life. "George has got himself a buckskin shirt and pants," this woman added. "He is gone hunting day and night."

It's easy for people in modern society to roman-
ticize Indian life, and it might well have been easy
for men like George as well. That impulse should be
guarded against. Virtually all of the Indian tribes
waged war against their neighbors and practiced
deeply sickening forms of torture. Prisoners who
weren't tomahawked on the spot could expect to be
disemboweled and tied to a tree with their own intes-
tines or blistered to death over a slow fire or simply
hacked to pieces and fed alive to the dogs. If there
is any conceivable defense for such cruelty, it might
be that in Europe at the time, the Spanish Inquisi-
tion was also busy serving up just as much barbarism
on behalf of the Catholic Church. Infidels were regularly burned alive, broken on the rack, sawn in half
lengthwise, or impaled slowly on wooden stakes from
the anus to the mouth. The Protestant Reformation
changed a lot of things about Christianity but not its
capacity for cruelty, and early Puritan leaders in New
England were also renowned for their harsh justice.
Cruelty, in other words, was very much the norm for
that era, and the native tribes of North America were
no exception.

On other levels, however, there seemed to be no
competing with the appeal of the Indians. Hunting

was obviously more varied and interesting than plowing fields. Sexual mores were more relaxed than in the early colonies (in the 1600s, colonial boys on Cape Cod were publicly whipped if they were caught talking to a girl they weren't related to). Indian clothing was more comfortable, Indian religion was less harsh, and Indian society was essentially classless and egalitarian. As the frontier marched across North America, from the Alleghenies to the Great Plains to the Rockies and then finally to the West Coast, successive generations of pioneers were subject to being captured and adopted into Indian tribes—or simply ran off to join them.

For all the temptations of native life, one of the most compelling might have been its fundamental egalitarianism. Personal property was usually limited to whatever could be transported by horse or on foot, so gross inequalities of wealth were difficult to accumulate. Successful hunters and warriors could support multiple wives, but unlike modern society, those advantages were generally not passed on through the generations. Social status came through hunting and war, which all men had access to, and women had far more autonomy and sexual freedom—and bore fewer children—than women in white society. "Here

I have no master," an anonymous colonial woman was quoted by the secretary of the French legation as saying about her life with the Indians. "I am the equal of all the women in the tribe, I do what I please without anyone's saying anything about it, I work only for myself, I shall marry if I wish and be unmarried again when I wish. Is there a single woman as independent as I in your cities?"

Because of these basic freedoms, tribal members tended to be exceedingly loyal. A white captive of the Kickapoo Nation who came to be known as John Dunn Hunter wrote that he had never heard of even a single instance of treason against the tribe, and as a result, punishments for such transgressions simply didn't exist. But cowardice was punished by death, as was murder within the tribe or any kind of communication with the enemy. It was a simple ethos that promoted loyalty and courage over all other virtues and considered the preservation of the tribe an almost sacred task.

Which indeed it was.

The question for Western society isn't so much why tribal life might be so appealing—it seems obvious on the face of it—but why Western society is so *un*appealing. On a material level it is clearly more comfortable and protected from the hardships of the natural world. But as societies become more affluent they tend to require more, rather than less, time and commitment by the individual, and it's possible that many people feel that affluence and safety simply aren't a good trade for freedom. One study in the 1960s found that nomadic !Kung people of the Kalahari Desert needed to work as little as twelve hours a week in order to survive—roughly one-quarter the hours of the average urban executive at the time. "The 'camp' is an open aggregate of cooperating persons which changes in size and composition from day to day," anthropologist Richard Lee noted with clear admiration in 1968. "The members move out each day to hunt and gather, and return in the evening to pool the collected foods in such a way that every person present receives an equitable share . . . Because of the strong emphasis on sharing, and the frequency of movement, surplus accumulation . . . is kept to a minimum."

The Kalahari is one of the harshest environments in the world, and the !Kung were able to continue living a Stone-Age existence well into the 1970s precisely because no one else wanted to live there. The !Kung were so well adapted to their environment that during times of drought, nearby farmers and cattle herders abandoned their livelihoods to join them in the bush because foraging and hunting were a more reliable source of food. The relatively relaxed pace of !Kung life—even during times of adversity—challenged long-standing ideas that modern society created a surplus of leisure time. It created exactly the opposite: a desperate cycle of work, financial obligation, and more work. The !Kung had far fewer belongings than Westerners, but their lives were under much greater personal control.

Among anthropologists, the !Kung are thought to present a fairly accurate picture of how our hominid ancestors lived for more than a million years before the advent of agriculture. Genetic adaptations take around 25,000 years to appear in humans, so the enormous changes that came with agriculture in the last 10,000 years have hardly begun to affect our gene pool. Early humans would most likely have lived in nomadic bands of around fifty people, much like the !Kung. They would have experienced high levels of accidental injuries and deaths. They would have countered domineering behavior by senior males by forming coalitions within the group. They would have been utterly intolerant of hoarding or selfishness. They would have occasionally endured episodes of hunger, violence, and hardship. They would have practiced extremely close and involved childcare. And they would have done almost everything in the company of others. They would have almost never been alone.

First agriculture, and then industry, changed two fundamental things about the human experience. The accumulation of personal property allowed people to make more and more individualistic choices about their lives, and those choices unavoidably diminished group efforts toward a common good. And as society modernized, people found themselves able to live independently from any communal group. A person living in a modern city or a suburb can, for the first time in history, go through an entire day—or an entire life—mostly encountering complete strangers. They can be surrounded by others and yet feel deeply, dangerously alone.

The evidence that this is hard on us is overwhelming. Although happiness is notoriously subjective and difficult to measure, mental illness is not. Numerous cross-cultural studies have shown that modern society—despite its nearly miraculous advances in medicine, science, and technology—is afflicted with some of the highest rates of depression, schizophrenia, poor health, anxiety, and chronic loneliness in human history. As affluence and urbanization rise in a society, rates of depression and suicide tend to go *up* rather than down. Rather than buffering people from clinical depression, increased wealth in a society seems to foster it.

Suicide is difficult to study among unacculturated tribal peoples because the early explorers who first encountered them rarely conducted rigorous ethnographic research. That said, there is remarkably little evidence of depression-based suicide in tribal societies. Among the American Indians, for example, suicide was understood to apply in very narrow circumstances: in old age to avoid burdening the tribe, in the ritual paroxysms of grief following the death of a spouse, in a hopeless but heroic battle with an enemy, and in an attempt to avoid the agony of torture. Among tribes that were ravaged by smallpox, it was also understood that a person whose face had been hideously disfigured by lesions might kill themselves. According to *The Ethics of Suicide: Historical Sources*, early chroniclers of the American Indians couldn't find any other examples of suicide that were rooted in psychological causes. Early sources report that the Bella Coola, the Ojibwa, the Montagnais, the Arapaho, the Plateau Yuma, the Southern Paiute, and the Zuni, among many others, experienced no suicide at all.

This stands in stark contrast to many modern societies, where the suicide rate is as high as 25 cases per 100,000 people. (In the United States, white middle-aged men currently have the highest rate at nearly 30 suicides per 100,000.) According to a global survey by the World Health Organization, people in wealthy countries suffer depression at as much as eight times the rate they do in poor countries, and people in countries with large income disparities— like the United States—run a much higher lifelong risk of developing severe mood disorders. A 2006 study comparing depression rates in Nigeria to depression rates in North America found that across the board, women in rural areas were less likely to get depressed than their urban counterparts. And urban North American women—the most affluent demographic of the study—were the *most* likely to experience depression.

The mechanism seems simple: poor people are

forced to share their time and resources more than wealthy people are, and as a result they live in closer communities. Inter-reliant poverty comes with its own stresses—and certainly isn't the American ideal—but it's much closer to our evolutionary heritage than affluence. A wealthy person who has never had to rely on help and resources from his community is leading a privileged life that falls way outside more than a million years of human experience. Financial independence can lead to isolation, and isolation can put people at a greatly increased risk of depression and suicide. This might be a fair trade for a generally wealthier society—but a trade it is.

The psychological effect of placing such importance on affluence can be seen in microcosm in the legal profession. In 2015, the *George Washington Law Review* surveyed more than 6,000 lawyers and found that conventional success in the legal profession—such as high billable hours or making partner at a law firm—had zero correlation with levels of happiness and well-being reported by the lawyers themselves. In fact, public defenders, who have far lower status than corporate lawyers, seem to lead significantly happier lives. The findings are in keeping with something called self-determination theory, which holds that human beings need three basic things in order to be content: they need to feel competent at what they do; they need to feel authentic in their lives; and they need to feel connected to others. These values are considered "intrinsic" to human happiness and far outweigh "extrinsic" values such as beauty, money, and status.

Bluntly put, modern society seems to emphasize extrinsic values over intrinsic ones, and as a result, mental health issues refuse to decline with growing wealth. The more assimilated a person is into American society, the more likely they are to develop depression during the course of their lifetime, regardless of what ethnicity they are. Mexicans born in the United States are wealthier than Mexicans born in Mexico but far more likely to suffer from depression. Like corporate lawyers, they may have a harder time achieving the three pillars of self-determination—autonomy, competence, and community—and wind up with a higher rate of depression. By contrast, Amish society has an exceedingly low rate of depression because, it is theorized, many Amish remain utterly unassimilated into modern society—to the extent that they won't even drive cars.

"The economic and marketing forces of modern society have engineered an environment...that maximize[s] consumption at the long-term cost of well-being," a study in the *Journal of Affective Disorders* concluded in 2012. "In effect, humans have dragged a body with a long hominid history into an overfed, malnourished, sedentary, sunlight-deficient, sleep-deprived, competitive, inequitable, and socially-isolating environment with dire consequences."

The alienating effects of wealth and modernity on the human experience start virtually at birth and never let up. Infants in hunter-gatherer societies are carried by their mothers as much as 90 percent of the time, which roughly corresponds to carrying rates among other primates. One can get an idea of how important this kind of touch is to primates from an infamous experiment conducted in the 1950s by a primatologist and psychologist named Harry Harlow. Baby rhesus monkeys were separated from their mothers and presented with the choice of two kinds of surrogates: a cuddly mother made out of terry cloth or an uninviting mother made out of wire mesh. The wire mesh mother, however, had a nipple that dispensed warm milk. The babies took their nourishment as quickly as possible and then rushed back to cling to the terry cloth mother, which had enough softness to provide the illusion of affection. Clearly, touch and closeness are vital to the health of baby primates—including humans.

In America during the 1970s, mothers maintained skin-to-skin contact with babies as little as 16 percent of the time, which is a level that traditional societies would probably consider a form of child abuse. Also unthinkable would be the modern practice of making young children sleep by themselves. In two American studies of middle-class families during the 1980s, 85 percent of young children slept alone in their own room—a figure that rose to 95 percent among families considered "well educated." Northern European societies, including America, are the only ones in history to make very young children sleep alone in such numbers. The isolation is thought to make many children bond intensely with stuffed animals for reassurance. Only in Northern European societies do children go through the well-known developmental stage of bonding with stuffed animals; elsewhere, children get their sense of safety from the adults sleeping near them.

The point of making children sleep alone, according to Western psychologists, is to make them "self-soothing," but that clearly runs contrary to our evolution. Humans are primates—we share 98 percent of our DNA with chimpanzees—and primates almost never leave infants unattended, because they would be extremely vulnerable to predators. Infants seem to know this instinctively, so being left alone in a dark room is terrifying to them. Compare the self-soothing approach to that of a traditional Mayan community in Guatemala: "Infants and children simply fall asleep when sleepy, do not wear specific sleep clothes or use traditional transitional objects, room share and cosleep with parents or siblings, and nurse on demand during the night." Another study notes about Bali: "Babies are encouraged to acquire quickly the capacity to sleep under any circumstances, including situations of high stimulation, musical performances, and other noisy observances which reflect their more complete integration into adult social activities."

As modern society reduced the role of community, it simultaneously elevated the role of authority. The two are uneasy companions, and as one goes up, the other tends to go down. In 2007, anthropologist Christopher Boehm published an analysis of 154 foraging societies that were deemed to be representative of our ancestral past, and one of their most common traits was the absence of major wealth disparities between individuals. Another was the absence of arbitrary authority. "Social life is politically egalitarian in that there is always a low tolerance by a group's mature males for one of their number dominating, bossing, or denigrating the others," Boehm observed. "The human conscience evolved in the Middle to Late Pleistocene as a result of . . . the hunting of large game. This required . . . cooperative band-level sharing of meat."

Because tribal foragers are highly mobile and can easily shift between different communities, authority is almost impossible to impose on the unwilling. And even without that option, males who try to take control of the group—or of the food supply—are often countered by coalitions of other males. This is clearly an ancient and adaptive behavior that tends to keep groups together and equitably cared for. In his survey of ancestral-type societies, Boehm found that—in addition to murder and theft—one of the most commonly punished infractions was "failure to share." Freeloading on the hard work of others and bullying were also high up on the list. Punishments included public ridicule, shunning, and, finally, "assassination of the culprit by the entire group."

A cave painting from the early Holocene in Spain shows ten figures with bows in their hands and a lone figure prone on the ground with what appear to be ten arrows sticking out of him. The configuration strongly suggests an execution rather than death in combat. Boehm points out that among current-day foraging groups, group execution is one of the most common ways of punishing males who try to claim a disproportionate amount of the group's resources.

Boehm's research has led him to believe that much of the evolutionary basis for moral behavior stems from group pressure. Not only are bad actions punished, but good actions are rewarded. When a person does something for another person—a prosocial act, as it's called—they are rewarded not only by group approval but also by an increase of dopamine and other pleasurable hormones in their blood. Group cooperation triggers higher levels of oxytocin, for example, which promotes everything from breast-feeding in women to higher levels of trust and group bonding in men. Both reactions impart a powerful sensation of well-being. Oxytocin creates a feedback loop of good-feeling and group loyalty that ultimately leads members to "self-sacrifice to promote group welfare," in the words of one study. Hominids that cooperated with one another—and punished those who didn't—must have outfought, outhunted, and outbred everyone else. These are the hominids that modern humans are descended from.

It's revealing, then, to look at modern society through the prism of more than a million years of human cooperation and resource sharing. Subsistence-level hunters aren't necessarily more moral than other people; they just can't get away with selfish behavior because they live in small groups where almost everything is open to scrutiny. Modern society, on the other hand, is a sprawling and anonymous mess where people can get away with incredible levels of dishonesty without getting caught. What tribal people would consider a profound betrayal of the group, modern society simply dismisses as fraud. Around 3 percent of people on unemployment assistance intentionally cheat the system, for example, which costs the United States more than $2 billion a year. Such abuse would be immediately punished in tribal society. Fraud in welfare and other entitlement programs is estimated to be at roughly the same rate, which adds another $1.5 billion in annual losses. That figure, however, is eclipsed by Medicare and Medicaid fraud, which is conservatively estimated at

10 percent of total payments—or around $100 billion a year. Some estimates run to two or three times that figure.

Fraud in the insurance industry is calculated to be $100 billion to $300 billion a year, a cost that gets passed directly to consumers in the form of higher premiums. All told, combined public- and private-sector fraud costs every household in the United States probably around $5,000 a year—or roughly the equivalent of working four months at a minimum-wage job. A hunter-gatherer community that lost four months' worth of food would face a serious threat to its survival, and its retribution against the people who caused that hardship would be immediate and probably very violent.

Westerners live in a complex society, and opportunities for scamming relatively small amounts of money off the bottom are almost endless—and very hard to catch. But scamming large amounts of money off the top seems even *harder* to catch. Fraud by American defense contractors is estimated at around $100 billion per year, and they are relatively well behaved compared to the financial industry. The FBI reports that since the economic recession of 2008, securities and commodities fraud in the United States has gone *up* by more than 50 percent. In the decade prior, almost 90 percent of corporate fraud cases—insider trading, kickbacks and bribes, false accounting—implicated the company's chief executive officer and/or chief financial officer. The recession, which was triggered by illegal and unwise banking practices, cost American shareholders several trillion dollars in stock value losses and is thought to have set the American economy back by a decade and a half. Total costs for the recession have been estimated to be as high as $14 trillion—or about $45,000 per citizen.

Most tribal and subsistence-level societies would inflict severe punishments on anyone who caused that kind of damage. Cowardice is another form of community betrayal, and most Indian tribes punished it with immediate death. (If that seems harsh, consider that the British military took "cowards" off the battlefield and executed them by firing squad as late as World War I.) It can be assumed that hunter-gatherers would treat their version of a welfare cheat or a dishonest banker as decisively as they would a coward. They may not kill him, but he would certainly be banished from the community. The fact that a group of people can cost American society several trillion dollars in losses—roughly one-quarter of that year's gross domestic product—and not be tried for high crimes shows how completely de-tribalized the country has become.

Dishonest bankers and welfare or insurance cheats are the modern equivalent of tribe members who quietly steal more than their fair share of meat or other resources. That is very different from alpha males who bully others and *openly* steal resources. Among hunter-gatherers, bullying males are often faced down by coalitions of other senior males, but that rarely happens in modern society. For years, the United States Securities and Exchange Commission has been trying to force senior corporate executives to disclose the ratio of their pay to that of their median employees. During the 1960s, senior executives in America typically made around twenty dollars for every dollar earned by a rank-and-file worker. Since then, that figure has climbed to 300-to-1 among S&P 500 companies, and in some cases it goes far higher than that. The US Chamber of Commerce managed to block all attempts to force disclosure of corporate pay ratios until 2015, when a weakened version of the rule was finally passed by the SEC in a strict party-line vote of three Democrats in favor and two Republicans opposed.

In hunter-gatherer terms, these senior executives

are claiming a disproportionate amount of food simply because they have the power to do so. A tribe like the !Kung would not permit that because it would represent a serious threat to group cohesion and survival, but that is not true for a wealthy country like the United States. There have been occasional demonstrations against economic disparity, like the Occupy Wall Street protest camp of 2011, but they were generally peaceful and ineffective. (The riots and demonstrations against racial discrimination that later took place in Ferguson, Missouri, and Baltimore, Maryland, led to changes in part because they attained a level of violence that threatened the civil order.) A deep and enduring economic crisis like the Great Depression of the 1930s, or a natural disaster that kills tens of thousands of people, might change America's fundamental calculus about economic justice. Until then, the American public will probably continue to refrain from broadly challenging both male and female corporate leaders who compensate themselves far in excess of their value to society.

That is ironic, because the political origins of the United States lay in confronting precisely this kind of resource seizure by people in power. King George

III of England caused the English colonies in America to rebel by trying to tax them without allowing them a voice in government. In this sense, democratic revolutions are just a formalized version of the sort of group action that coalitions of senior males have used throughout the ages to confront greed and abuse. Thomas Paine, one of the principal architects of American democracy, wrote a formal denunciation of civilization in a tract called *Agrarian Justice*: "Whether ... civilization has most promoted or most injured the general happiness of man is a question that may be strongly contested," he wrote in 1795. "[Both] the most affluent and the most miserable of the human race are to be found in the countries that are called civilized."

When Paine wrote his tract, Shawnee and Delaware warriors were still attacking settlements just a few hundred miles from downtown Philadelphia. They held scores of white captives, many of whom had been adopted into the tribe and had no desire to return to colonial society. There is no way to know the effect on Paine's thought process of living next door to a communal Stone-Age society, but it might have been crucial. Paine acknowledged that these tribes lacked the advantages of the arts and science and manufacturing, and yet they lived in a society where personal poverty was unknown and the natural rights of man were actively-promoted.

In that sense, Paine claimed, the American Indian should serve as a model for how to eradicate poverty and bring natural rights back into civilized life.

WAR MAKES YOU AN ANIMAL

LIKE A LOT OF BOYS I PLAYED WAR WHEN I WAS YOUNG, and like a lot of men I retained an intense and abiding curiosity about it. And like a lot of people, my family was deeply affected by war and probably wouldn't have existed without it. One of my mother's ancestors emigrated from Germany in order to fight in the American Revolution and was given a land grant in Ohio in return. His last name was Grimm; he was related to the great folklorists who recorded German fairy tales. One of Grimm's descendants married into another frontier family, the Carrolls, who were almost wiped out by Indians during a raid on their remote Pennsylvania homestead in 1781. The Carroll wife managed to hide in a cornfield with her four-year-old son, James, while the Indians killed her two teenage sons and her dog. The husband was off in town that day. I'm descended from James.

My father was half Jewish and grew up in Europe. He was thirteen when his family fled the Spanish Civil War and settled in Paris, and seventeen when they left Paris ahead of the German army and emigrated to the United States. He tried to sign up for military service but was turned down due to asthma, so he eventually helped the war effort by working on jet engines in Paterson, New Jersey. Later he got a degree in fluid mechanics and worked on submarine design. When I turned eighteen I received my selective service card in the mail, in case the United States needed to draft me, and I declared that I wasn't going to sign it. The Vietnam War had just ended and every adult I knew had been against it. I had no problem, personally, with fighting a war; I just didn't trust my government to send me to one that was completely necessary.

My father's reaction surprised me. Vietnam had made him vehemently antiwar, so I expected him to applaud my decision, but instead he told me that American soldiers had saved the world from fascism during World War II and that thousands of young

Americans were buried in his homeland of France. "You don't owe your country *nothing*," I remember him telling me. "You owe it something, and depending on what happens, you might owe it your life."

The way my father put it completely turned the issue around for me: suddenly the draft card wasn't so much an obligation as a chance to be part of something bigger than myself. And he'd made it clear that if the United States embarked on a war that I felt was wrong, I could always refuse to go; in his opinion, protesting an immoral war was just as honorable as fighting a moral one. Either way, he made it clear that my country needed help protecting the principles and ideals that I'd benefited from my entire life.

In many tribal societies, young men had to prove themselves by undergoing initiation rites that demonstrated their readiness for adulthood. In some tribes, such as the Mara of northern Australia, the tests were so brutal that initiates occasionally died. Those who refused or failed these tests weren't considered men and led their lives in a kind of gender twilight. Modern society obviously doesn't conduct initiations on its young men, but many boys still do their best to demonstrate their readiness for manhood in all kinds of clumsy and dangerous ways. They drive too fast, get into fights, haze each other, play sports, join fraternities, drink too much, and gamble with their lives in a million idiotic ways. Girls generally don't take those kinds of risks, and as a result, boys in modern society die by violence and accidents at many times the rate that girls do. These deaths can be thought of as one generation after another trying to run their own initiation rites because they live in a society that no longer does that for them. To the extent that boys are drawn to war, it may be less out of an interest in violence than a longing for the kind of maturity and respect that often come with it.

That, at any rate, was how I came to understand my own curiosity about combat when I was young. That was how I came to understand why I found myself, broke and directionless, on the tarmac of the Sarajevo airport at age thirty-one, listening to the tapping of machine-gun fire in a nearby suburb named Dobrinja.

Sarajevo was under siege by Serb forces that had overrun most of Bosnia during the civil war that started when the former Yugoslavia broke apart in 1991. I had almost no experience as a journalist, but going to a war was surprisingly easy: I flew to Vienna, took a train to Zagreb, and pulled into a station that had field guns lined up on flatbed carriages and soldiers standing around with long knives in their belts. It was a soft summer night and the atmosphere felt electric—exactly what I'd been looking for since I was a teenager. I took the same backpack that I'd had out West a decade earlier, and in it I'd put a block of field notebooks, a box of pens, a manual typewriter, and a change of clothes. I'd heard there was no electricity in Sarajevo, so the typewriter would guarantee that I could always write and file assignments if I were lucky enough to get any. I also had a sleeping bag and a letter from a magazine editor whom I'd convinced to vouch for me so that I could at least get a press pass when I arrived.

I eventually got into Sarajevo on a UN relief flight from Italy. Sarajevo had once been a gorgeous Hapsburg-era city filled with cafés, art galleries, and theaters, but now it was sweltering in the July heat and permeated by the smell of burning garbage. Destroyed cars littered intersections where street battles had taken place, and almost every building was spattered with shrapnel. The bombed-out *Oslobodjenje* newspaper building oozed its guts out a lower floor as if someone had just pulled a huge plug on the inside. People hired taxis to drive close to the front lines so they could talk by radio to friends on the other side, who were also in taxis. At night the city was completely, absolutely dark and you could walk through it as if you were the only human left on earth. During the day, the streets were filled with people carrying jugs of water or dragging branches for firewood or walking to work in their office clothes, some semblance of life the way it was before. Open areas around apartment buildings had been planted with summer vegetables, and there was even a little turbine made out of tin cans and a bicycle wheel in the Miljacka River that could charge a car battery in a day.

The city stretched east to west along a narrow valley surrounded by mountains, and once the Serbs took the high ground—which they did almost immediately—it was close to indefensible. Tanks could drill buildings with flat-trajectory shots that easily punched through exterior walls, and mortars shrieked down into places, like courtyards, that seemed otherwise protected. Snipers took up positions on the steep hillsides south of the Miljacka and around the nearly encircled suburb of Dobrinja and dropped civilians at will. It was not uncommon to see the body of an older person crumpled in the street with a bullet in their forehead and the contents of a shopping bag spilled out over the pavement. A public spectacle until dark, when someone could run out and pull the body off the street.

The Serbs controlled every road out of the city and most of the mountaintops around it and allowed just enough food in to keep people alive. The Serb mafia did business across the front lines with the Sarajevo mafia—who also fought to defend the city—and both made an enormous amount of money. A main road that ran the length of the city was so exposed to gunfire that it became known as Sniper Alley. The few people with cars drove at seventy miles an hour on gas that cost fifty dollars a gallon, and still, many of them didn't make it. A year into the siege the Bosnians dug a tunnel under no-man's-land at the airport, but until then, the only way out of the city was to sprint across the runway past Serb machine-gun positions. A lot of those people didn't make it, either. Every morning, French UN troops at the airport would drive out in armored personnel carriers to pick up the bodies.

Over the course of the three-year siege almost 70,000 people were killed or wounded by Serb forces shooting into the city—roughly 20 percent of the population. The United Nations estimated that half of the children in the city had seen someone killed in front of them, and about one in five had lost a family member in the war. People intentionally exposed themselves to snipers just to be put out of their misery. One year into the siege, just before I got to the city, a teenage couple walked into no-man's-land along the Miljacka River, trying to cross into a Serb-held area. They were quickly gunned down, the young man falling first and the woman crawling over to him as she died. He was a Serb and she was a Muslim, and they had been in love all through high school. They lay there for days because the area was too dangerous for anyone to retrieve their bodies.

I saw a lot of strange things in that city, the kinds of contortions that only war can bring to a people, but maybe the most startling was this: a middle-aged man in a business suit crouched over some small project in the courtyard of a modern high-rise. The building could have been any bank or insurance company in Europe, except that the windows were blown out and the walls were scarred with shrapnel. I looked closer and saw that the man was arranging dead twigs into a pile. When he was done, he positioned an aluminum pot on top of the pile and lit the twigs with a cigarette lighter. Then he stood up and looked at me.

If there's an image of the Apocalypse, I thought, it might be a man in a business suit building a fire in the courtyard of an abandoned high-rise. In different circumstances it could be any of us, anywhere, but it had happened to him here, and there wasn't much I could do about it. I nodded to him and he nodded back and then I left him in peace.

The one thing that might be said for societal collapse is that—for a while at least—everyone is equal. In 1915 an earthquake killed 30,000 people in Avezzano, Italy, in less than a minute. The worst-hit areas had a mortality rate of 96 percent. The rich were killed along with the poor, and virtually everyone who survived was immediately thrust into the most basic struggle for survival: they needed food, they needed water, they needed shelter, and they needed to rescue the living and bury the dead. In that sense, plate tectonics under the town of Avezzano managed to recreate the communal conditions of our evolutionary past quite well. "An earthquake achieves what the law promises but does not in practice maintain," one of the survivors wrote. "The equality of all men."

As Thomas Paine labored to articulate his goals for a free society, he could have easily taken his inspiration from earthquake survivors instead of from the American Indians. Communities that have been devastated by natural or man-made disasters almost never lapse into chaos and disorder; if anything, they become more just, more egalitarian, and more deliberately fair to individuals. (Despite erroneous news reports, New Orleans experienced a *drop* in crime rates after Hurricane Katrina, and much of the "looting" turned out to be people looking for food.) The kinds of community-oriented behaviors that typically occur after a natural disaster are exactly the virtues that Paine was hoping to promote in his revolutionary tracts.

The question of societal breakdown in the face of calamity suddenly became urgent in the run-up to World War II, when the world powers were anticipating aerial bombardments deliberately calculated to cause mass hysteria in the cities. English authorities, for example, predicted that German attacks would produce 35,000 casualties a day in London alone (total civilian casualties for the country were not even twice that). No one knew how a civilian population would react to that kind of trauma, but the Churchill government assumed the worst. So poor was their opinion of the populace—particularly the working-class people of East London—that emergency planners were reluctant to even build public bomb shelters because they worried people would move into them and simply never move out. Economic production would plummet and the shelters themselves, it was feared, would become a breeding ground for political dissent and even Communism.

Nothing could have been further from the truth. "We would really have all gone down onto the beaches with broken bottles," one woman remembered of the public's determination to fight the Germans. "We would have done anything—*anything*—to stop them." On September 7, 1940, German bombers started hitting London in earnest and did not let up until the following May. For fifty-seven consecutive days, waves of German bombers flew over London and dropped thousands of tons of high explosives directly into residential areas, killing hundreds of people at a time. Throughout the Blitz, as it was known, many Londoners trudged to work in the morning, trudged across town to shelters or tube stations in the evening, and then trudged back to work again when it got light. Conduct was so good in the shelters that volunteers never even had to summon the police to maintain order. If anything, the crowd policed themselves according to unwritten rules that made life bearable for complete strangers jammed shoulder to shoulder on floors that were at times awash in urine.

"Ten thousand people had come together without ties of friendship or economics, with no plans at all as to what they meant to do," one man wrote about life in a massive concrete structure known as Tilbury Shelter. "They found themselves, literally overnight, inhabitants of a vague twilight town of strangers. At first there were no rules, rewards or penalties, no hierarchy or command. Almost immediately, 'laws' began to emerge—laws enforced not by police and wardens (who at first proved helpless in the face of such multitudes) but by the shelterers themselves."

Eight million men, women, and children in Greater London endured the kind of aerial bombardment that even soldiers are rarely subjected to. Often the badly wounded were just given morphine and left to die in the rubble while rescue crews moved on to people they thought they could save. The tempo of the bombing was so intense, one woman recalled, that it sounded like an enormous marching band stomping around the city. Another recounted being flattened by an explosion and finding herself "clutching the floor as if it were a cliff face that I had to hang onto." A food manufacturing plant named Hartley's was bombed and the dead were carried out covered in marmalade. A hat factory was hit and the dead were brought out bristling with sewing needles. One underground shelter took a direct hit and 600 people were killed instantly. Another was hit by a bomb that severed a water main, and more than 100 people died when their shelter flooded in minutes.

On and on the horror went, people dying in their homes or neighborhoods while doing the most mundane things. Not only did these experiences fail to produce mass hysteria, they didn't even trigger much individual psychosis. Before the war, projections for psychiatric breakdown in England ran as high as four million people, but as the Blitz progressed, psychiatric hospitals around the country saw admissions go *down*. Emergency services in London reported an average of only two cases of "bomb neuroses" a week. Psychiatrists watched in puzzlement as long-standing patients saw their symptoms subside during the period of intense air raids. Voluntary admissions to psychiatric wards noticeably declined, and even epileptics reported having fewer seizures. "Chronic neurotics of peacetime now drive ambulances," one doctor remarked. Another ventured to suggest that some people actually did *better* during wartime.

The positive effects of war on mental health were first noticed by the great sociologist Emile Durkheim, who found that when European countries went to war, suicide rates dropped. Psychiatric wards in Paris were strangely empty during both world wars, and that remained true even as the German army rolled into the city in 1940. Researchers documented a similar phenomenon during civil wars in Spain, Algeria, Lebanon, and Northern Ireland. An Irish psychologist named H. A. Lyons found that suicide rates in Belfast dropped 50 percent during the riots of 1969 and 1970, and homicide and other violent crimes also went down. Depression rates for both men and women declined abruptly during that period, with men experiencing the most extreme drop in the most violent districts. County Derry, on the other hand— which suffered almost no violence at all—saw male depression rates *rise* rather than fall. Lyons hypothesized that men in the peaceful areas were depressed because they couldn't help their society by participating in the struggle.

"When people are actively engaged in a cause their lives have more purpose . . . with a resulting improvement in mental health," Lyons wrote in the *Journal of Psychosomatic Research* in 1979. "It would be irresponsible to suggest violence as a means of improving mental health, but the Belfast findings suggest that people will feel better psychologically if they have more involvement with their community."

During the London Blitz, the sheer regularity of the air raids seemed to provide its own weird reassurance, and the intense racket of the antiaircraft batteries—however ineffective—helped keep Londoners from feeling completely vulnerable. The total amount of beer consumed in the city did not change much, and neither did the rate of church attendance. People did resort to superstition and magic, however, carrying talismans or sprigs of heather and refusing, for some reason, to wear green. One woman felt that the Germans were targeting her specifically and would go out only if she could blend into a crowd. Another man found his service pistol from the First World War and tried to teach his wife how to kill Germans with it. Men reported smoking more.

Women reported feeling depressed more—though statistically, they attempted suicide less. In March 1941, perhaps in an attempt to demystify the enemy, British authorities deposited a German Junkers 88 dive bomber in one of the most severely damaged neighborhoods of Plymouth. The plane sat there— unlabeled, unguarded, and unexplained—while citizens wandered up to examine it and observers quietly took notes.

"The overwhelming effect was of mild pleasure, interest, and relief," one researcher noted of people's reactions. "Men were more interested in the material, engine, craftsmanship, all of which were elaborately praised. Women noticed especially the size. Some evidently thought of an enemy bomber as a remote thing, a specter in the sky...the reality was some- how reassuring, almost friendly."

The reactions of thousands of civilians to the stresses of war were recorded in detail by something known as Mass-Observation, which was a mostly volunteer corps of Britons who were asked to observe their countrymen "as if they were birds." Some vol- unteers went out every day and wrote down every- thing they saw or heard; others were told to keep journals and to fill out questionnaires about their experiences and feelings. The project proved controversial because it documented what was already obvious: the air raids failed to trigger the kind of mass hysteria that government officials had predicted. That, ironically, was an unwelcome bit of news once the tide of war had turned and Allied forces adopted the same strategy of apocalyptic air raids against the Germans.

The Blitz, as bad as it was, paled in comparison to what the Allies did. Dresden lost more people in one night than London did during the entire war. Firestorms engulfed whole neighborhoods and used up so much oxygen that people who were untouched by the blasts reportedly died of asphyxiation instead. Fully a third of the German population was subjected to bombardment, and around one million people were killed or wounded. American analysts based in England monitored the effects of the bombing to see if any cracks began to appear in the German resolve, and to their surprise found exactly the opposite: the more the Allies bombed, the more defiant the German population became. Industrial production actually *rose* in Germany during the war. And the cities with the highest morale were the ones—like Dresden— that were bombed the hardest. According to German psychologists who compared notes with their American counterparts after the war, it was the untouched cities where civilian morale suffered the most. Thirty years later, H. A. Lyons would document an almost identical phenomenon in riot-torn Belfast.

The United States Strategic Bombing Survey posted observers in England to evaluate the effectiveness of their strategy, and one of them, Charles Fritz, became an open critic of the rationale behind the bombing campaign. Intrigued by the fact that in both England and Germany, civilian resilience had risen in response to the air raids, Fritz went on to complete a more general study of how communities respond to calamity. After the war he turned his attention to natural disasters in the United States and formulated a broad theory about social resilience. He was unable to find a single instance where communities that had been hit by catastrophic events lapsed into sustained panic, much less anything approaching anarchy. If anything, he found that social bonds were reinforced during disasters, and that people overwhelmingly devoted their energies toward the good of the community rather than just themselves.

In 1961, Fritz assembled his ideas into a lengthy paper that began with the startling sentence, "Why do large-scale disasters produce such mentally healthy conditions?" His data was compiled by a team of twenty-five researchers who worked for the National Opinion Research Center, based at the University of Chicago. Their job was to rush to disaster sites and interview the inhabitants about how they were adapting to their new circumstances; by 1959, NORC researchers had compiled roughly 9,000 survivor interviews. Fritz also scoured academic publications for anything related to natural or man-made disasters. His study was conducted during the height of the Cold War, when the Russian nuclear threat was foremost in the minds of civil defense planners. Never mentioned in the report—though impossible to ignore—is the possibility that the study was intended to assess whether the United States could continue to function after a nuclear exchange with Russia.

Fritz's theory was that modern society has gravely disrupted the social bonds that have always characterized the human experience, and that disasters thrust people back into a more ancient, organic way of relating. Disasters, he proposed, create a "community of sufferers" that allows individuals to experience an immensely reassuring connection to others. As people come together to face an existential threat, Fritz found, class differences are temporarily erased, income disparities become irrelevant, race is overlooked, and individuals are assessed simply by what they are willing to do for the group. It is a kind of fleeting social utopia that, Fritz felt, is enormously gratifying to the average person and downright therapeutic to people suffering from mental illness.

Fritz's conclusions were later borne out in a study of the city of Yungay, in central Chile, which was struck by a devastating earthquake and rockslide on May 31, 1970. Ninety percent of the population of Yungay died almost instantly, and 70,000 people were killed throughout the region—roughly equivalent to a nuclear strike on that area. The rockslide that buried the city put so much dust into the air that helicopters couldn't land, and the survivors of Yungay were left completely on their own for days. Into this terrifying vacuum, a new social order quickly sprang up. "Concepts of individual private property temporarily submerged," anthropologist Anthony Oliver-Smith later wrote in his paper "Brotherhood of Pain." "The crisis also had an immediate status-leveling effect on the nascent community of survivors it had created. A sense of brotherhood... prevailed as Indian and *mestizo*, lower and upper class, collaborated in the collective efforts to obtain immediate necessities and survive."

As soon as relief flights began delivering aid to the area, class divisions returned and the sense of brotherhood disappeared. The modern world had arrived.

If there are phrases that characterize the life of our early ancestors, "community of sufferers" and "brotherhood of pain" surely must come close. Their lives were probably less labor-intensive than lives in modern society, as demonstrated by the !Kung, but the mortality rate would have been much higher. The advantages of group cooperation would include far more effective hunting and defense, and groups that failed to function cooperatively must have gradually died out. Adaptive behavior tends to be reinforced hormonally, emotionally, and culturally, and one can see all three types of adaptation at work in people who act on behalf of others.

Humans are so strongly wired to help one another—and enjoy such enormous social benefits from doing so—that people regularly risk their lives for complete strangers. That risk-taking tends to express itself in very different ways in men and in women.

Men perform the vast majority of bystander rescues, and children, the elderly, and women are the most common recipients of them. Children are helped regardless of gender, as are the elderly, but women of reproductive age are twice as likely to be helped by a stranger than men are. Men have to wait, on average, until age seventy-five before they can expect the same kind of assistance in a life-threatening situation that women get their whole lives. Given the disproportionately high value of female reproduction to any society, risking male lives to save female lives makes enormous evolutionary sense. According to a study based on a century of records at the Carnegie Hero Fund Commission, male bystanders performed more than 90 percent of spontaneous rescues of strangers, and around one in five were killed in the attempt. ("Hero" is generally defined as risking your life to save non-kin from mortal danger. The resulting mortality rate is higher than for most US combat units.) Researchers theorize that greater upper-body strength and a predominantly male personality trait known as "impulsive sensation seeking" lead men to overwhelmingly dominate this form of extreme caretaking.

But women are more likely than men to display

something called moral courage. The Righteous Among the Nations is an award given to non-Jews who helped save Jewish lives during the Holocaust and by its very nature selects for people who have a deep moral conviction about right and wrong. In Poland, the Netherlands, and France, providing refuge to Jews who were trying to evade the German authorities was a crime punishable by death, and while the decision to do so didn't require the same kind of muscular action that men excel at, it could be just as deadly.

There are more than 20,000 names in the Righteous Among the Nations records, and an analysis conducted in 2004 found that if married couples are excluded, women slightly outnumber men in the list of people who risked their lives to help Jews. The greater empathic concern women demonstrate for others may lead them to take positions on moral or social issues that men are less likely to concern themselves with. Women tend to act heroically within their own moral universe, regardless of whether anyone else knows about it—donating more kidneys to nonrelatives than men do, for example. Men, on the other hand, are far more likely to risk their lives at a moment's notice, and that reaction is particularly strong when others are watching, or when they are part of a group.

In late 2015, a bus in eastern Kenya was stopped by gunmen from an extremist group named Al-Shabaab that made a practice of massacring Christians as part of a terrorism campaign against the Western-aligned Kenyan government. The gunmen demanded that Muslim and Christian passengers separate themselves into two groups so that the Christians could be killed, but the Muslims—most of whom were women—refused to do it. They told the gunmen that they would all die together if necessary, but that the Christians would not be singled out for execution. The Shabaab eventually let everyone go.

Sexual division of risk-taking would seem to suit the human race particularly well. We evolved, and continue to exist, in a physical world that assaults us with threats, but we also depend on a strong sense of morality and social justice to keep our communities intact. And intact communities are far more likely to survive than fragmented ones. When a woman gives shelter to a family because she doesn't want to raise her children in a world where people can be massacred because of their race or their beliefs, she is taking a huge risk but also promoting the kind of moral thinking that has clearly kept hominid communities glued together for hundreds of thousands of years. It is exactly the same kind of altruistic choice—with all the attendant risks and terrors—that a man makes when he runs into a burning building to save someone else's children. Both are profound acts of selflessness that distinguish us from all other mammals, including the higher primates that we are so closely related to.

The beauty and the tragedy of the modern world is that it eliminates many situations that require people to demonstrate a commitment to the collective good. Protected by police and fire departments and relieved of most of the challenges of survival, an urban man might go through his entire life without having to come to the aid of someone in danger—or even give up his dinner. Likewise, a woman in a society that has codified its moral behavior into a set of laws and penalties might never have to make a choice that puts her very life at risk. What would you risk dying for—and for whom—is perhaps the most profound question a person can ask themselves. The vast majority of people in modern society are able to pass their whole lives without ever having to answer that question, which is both an enormous blessing and a significant loss. It is a loss because having to face that question has, for tens of millennia, been one of the ways that we have defined ourselves as people. And it is a blessing because life has gotten far less difficult and traumatic than it was for most people even a century ago.

The gender differentiation of courage during life-and-death situations is so vital to group survival that it seems to get duplicated even within same-sex groups. Like most dangerous jobs, coal mining is an almost exclusively male activity that generally draws its workers from a particularly undereducated, blue-collar population. Disasters happen with appalling regularity in the industry, and when they do, groups of men are often trapped miles underground for days or weeks at a time. These incidents have offered social scientists a way to examine how men react to danger and organize themselves to maximize their chances of survival.

At 8:05 on the evening of October 23, 1958, the Springhill Mine in Nova Scotia experienced what coal miners know as a "bump": a sudden contraction and settling of sedimentary layers deep underground that generates the forces of a massive explosion throughout the complex. Springhill was one of the deepest coal mines in the world, and the bump of 1958 was so powerful that it was felt 800 miles away. There were 174 men in the mine at the time, and 74 were killed immediately as strata compressed and the passageways collapsed. Of the survivors, 81 men were able to make their way to safety and 19 found themselves trapped more than 12,000 feet down the mine shafts. Several were badly injured, and two were pinned by debris and unable to move.

The men had almost no food or water and only a few days' worth of battery power in their headlamps. There was a group of six miners in one area, a group of twelve in another, and a lone miner who was partially buried at a third location. There was no contact between the groups and no way for them to communicate with the outside world. Within minutes of the bump, off-duty miners and specially trained draegermen were converging on the mine. Draegermen wear gas masks and breathing apparatus—invented by a German named Alexander Dräger—that allow them to survive the methane and carbon dioxide gas that seep out of coal strata. Another group, "barefaced miners," can work harder and faster than the draegermen but have to be confined to areas that don't have any gas.

The rescuers began digging their way through

the collapsed passageways, working in spaces so cramped that they were forced to cut the handles off their pickaxes in order to swing them. Even a strong man could last no more than three or four minutes on a pickax in such circumstances, so they worked in four-man teams and kept rotating positions so that "the pick never stopped," as one report put it. After several days, they started digging past the crushed bodies of dead miners. The effect of encountering a putrefying body in the close confines of the passageways was devastating, and almost everyone vomited when they encountered one. Often the dead were known personally to the men who were digging them out. Some rescuers couldn't take the psychological trauma and asked to be taken off the job, and others were able to suppress their reactions and continue digging. There was no dishonor for those who couldn't take it and tremendous admiration for those who could.

"The miners' code of rescue meant that each trapped miner had the knowledge that he would never be buried alive if it were humanly possible for his friends to reach him," a 1960 study called *Individual and Group Behavior in a Coal Mine Disaster* explained. "At the same time, the code was not rigid enough to ostracize those who could not face the rescue role."

Meanwhile, two miles down the mine shaft, nineteen men sat in absolute darkness trying to figure out what to do. One of the groups included a man whose arm had been pinned between two timbers, and, out of earshot, the others discussed whether to amputate it or not. The man kept begging them to, but they decided against it and he eventually died. Both groups ran out of food and water and started to drink their own urine. Some used coal dust or bark from the timbers to mask the taste. Some were so hungry that they tried to eat chunks of coal as well. There was an unspoken prohibition against crying, though some men allowed themselves to quietly break down after the lamps died, and many of them avoided thinking about their families. Mostly they just thought about neutral topics like hunting. One man obsessed over the fact that he owed $1.40 for a car part and hoped his wife would pay it after he died.

Almost immediately, certain men stepped into leadership roles. While there was still lamplight, these men scouted open passageways to see if they could escape and tried to dig through rockfalls that were blocking their path. When they ran out of water, one man went in search of more and managed to find a precious gallon, which he distributed to the others. These men were also instrumental in getting their fellow survivors to start drinking their own urine or trying to eat coal. Canadian psychologists who interviewed the miners after their rescue determined that these early leaders tended to lack empathy and emotional control, that they were not concerned with the opinions of others, that they associated with only one or two other men in the group, and that their physical abilities far exceeded their verbal abilities. But all of these traits allowed them to take forceful, life-saving action where many other men might not.

Once the escape attempts failed, different kinds of leaders emerged. In what researchers termed the "survival period," the ability to wait in complete darkness without giving up hope or succumbing to panic became crucial. Researchers determined that the leaders during this period were entirely focused on group morale and used skills that were diametrically opposed to those of the men who had led the escape attempts. They were highly sensitive to people's moods, they intellectualized things in order to meet group needs, they reassured the men who were starting to give up hope, and they worked hard to be accepted by the entire group.

Without exception, men who were leaders during one period were almost completely inactive during the other; no one, it seemed, was suited to both roles. These two kinds of leaders more or less correspond to the male and female roles that emerge spontaneously in open society during catastrophes such as earthquakes or the Blitz. They reflect an ancient duality that is masked by the ease and safety of modern life but that becomes immediately apparent when disasters strike. If women aren't present to provide the empathic leadership that every group needs, certain men will do it. If men aren't present to take immediate action in an emergency, women will step in. (Almost all the female Carnegie Hero award recipients acted in situations where there were no men present.) To some degree the sexes are interchangeable—meaning they can easily be substituted for one another—but gender roles aren't. Both are necessary for the healthy functioning of society, and those roles will always be filled regardless of whether both sexes are available to do it.

The coming-together that societies often experience during catastrophes is usually temporary, but sometimes the effect can last years or even decades. British historians have linked the hardships of the Blitz—and the social unity that followed—to a landslide vote that brought the Labour Party into power in 1945 and eventually gave the United Kingdom national health care and a strong welfare state. The Blitz hit after years of poverty in England, and both experiences served to bind the society together in ways that rejected the primacy of business interests over the welfare of the people. That era didn't end until the wartime generation started to fade out and Margaret Thatcher was elected prime minister in 1979. "In every upheaval we rediscover humanity and regain freedoms," one sociologist wrote about England's reaction to the war. "We relearn some old truths about the connection between happiness, unselfishness, and the simplification of living."

What catastrophes seem to do—sometimes in the span of a few minutes—is turn back the clock on ten thousand years of social evolution. Self-interest gets subsumed into group interest because there is no survival outside group survival, and that creates a social bond that many people sorely miss.

Twenty years after the end of the siege of Sarajevo, I returned to find people talking a little sheepishly about how much they longed for those days. More precisely, they longed for *who they'd been* back then. Even my taxi driver on the ride from the airport told me that during the war, he'd been in a special unit that slipped through the enemy lines to help other besieged enclaves. "And now look at me," he said, dismissing the dashboard with a wave of his hand.

For a former soldier to miss the clarity and importance of his wartime duty is one thing, but for civilians to is quite another. "Whatever I say about war, I still hate it," one survivor, Nidžara Ahmetašević, made sure to tell me after I'd interviewed her about the nostalgia of her generation. "I do miss something from the war. But I also believe that the world we are living in—and the peace that we have—is very fucked up if somebody is missing war. And many people do."

Ahmetašević is now a prominent Bosnian journalist who has dedicated her life to understanding the war crimes that blossomed all around her when she was young. She was seventeen when the war broke out, and within weeks had been hit by shrapnel from an artillery round that crashed into her parents' apartment. She was rushed to the hospital and underwent reconstructive surgery to her severely damaged leg without anesthesia. ("They hold you down and you scream," she said when I asked about the pain. "That helps.") The hospital was overflowing with wounded—they were laid out in the toilets, in the hallways, in the entranceways—and the staff didn't even have the time to change blood-soaked sheets after people died. They just loaded the next person onto the bed and continued working. The first night, an old woman died next to Ahmetašević and somehow rolled onto her in her final agonies. Ahmetašević woke in the morning to find the woman on top of her, the first of many bodies she would see during the war.

After two weeks Ahmetašević was finally sent back to her parents' apartment on crutches and resumed what passed as normal life during wartime. Her neighborhood had organized five apartment buildings—perhaps sixty families—into a huge cooperative that shared food and ovens and shelter. Vegetable gardens were planted around the buildings and everyone ate from the food they produced. Water was gathered individually from roof gutters or from hand pumps in town, but virtually everything else was shared. On her eighteenth birthday, Ahmetašević remembers being given a single egg by one of her neighbors. She couldn't figure out how to share it with her friends, so she decided to use the egg to make pancakes so that everyone could have some.

The basement of one of the buildings was deep enough to serve as a bomb shelter, and teenagers from the neighborhood led a kind of communal life down there that was almost entirely separate from the adults above ground. The boys would go off to fight on the front line for ten days at a stretch and then return to join the girls, who lived down there full-time. Everyone slept on mattresses on the floor together and ate their meals together and fell in and out of love together and played music and talked about literature and joked about the war. "The boys were like our brothers," Ahmetašević said. "It's not like we girls were waiting for them and crying . . . no, we had a party. To be honest, it was a kind of liberation. The love that we shared was enormous. They'd come from the front lines and most of them were musicians and they would have small concerts for us. We didn't believe in heroes. We were punk rockers. Our biggest hero was David Bowie."

Six months into the siege, Ahmetašević's parents managed to get her evacuated to Italy because they weren't sure she was going to survive. She had lost a lot of weight after her surgery and never managed to put it back on. Although she was safe in Italy, and finally healing from her wounds, the loneliness she felt was unbearable. She was worried that if the war never stopped, everyone would be killed and she would be left alone in the world. She finally started trying to figure out how to get back into Sarajevo—something that almost no one did. From a bureaucratic standpoint it was even harder than getting out of the besieged city, but with her mother's help, she finally did it. She flew into the blown-up, sandbagged airport and hitched a ride into town and back to her family.

"I missed being that close to people, I missed being loved in that way," she told me. "In Bosnia—as it is now—we don't trust each other anymore; we became really bad people. We didn't learn the lesson of the war, which is how important it is to share everything you have with human beings close to you. The best way to explain it is that the war makes you an animal. We were animals. It's insane—but that's the basic human instinct, to help another human being who is sitting or standing or lying close to you."

I asked Ahmetašević if people had ultimately been happier during the war.

"We were *the happiest*," Ahmetašević said. Then she added: "And we laughed more."

IN BITTER SAFETY
I AWAKE

———

THE FIRST TIME I REALIZED I HAD A PROBLEM, I WAS in a subway station in New York City. It was almost a year before the attacks of 9/11 and I'd just come back from two months in Afghanistan with Ahmed Shah Massoud, the leader of the Northern Alliance. I had no appreciation for how that experience would affect me psychologically, and so I was completely unprepared for the aftermath. Massoud was fighting a desperate action to open up supply lines across the Amu Darya River before winter set in, and he was blocked by Taliban positions on a prominent ridge overlooking the Tajik border. Hundreds of Taliban troops were dug in with tanks and artillery and protected by a few MiG jets that were based at Taloqan. Al Qaeda's infamous

71

055 commando brigade was up there, as well as volunteers from Uzbekistan and Chechnya, and Pakistani commanders who shouted over the radio in Urdu and berated the locals for not fighting hard enough.

Massoud's men were outnumbered three to one and in short supply of everything from tank rounds to food. At one point I and the men I was with made our way to a frontline position that had just been taken from the Taliban and arrived in time for the inevitable counterattack. We curled up in the slit trenches and listened to rockets come screaming in and detonate against the packed-clay earth. The Northern Alliance had no artillery to speak of, so all we could do was stay down and wait for the Taliban to run out of rockets. We eventually managed to get out of there, though we lost one of our packhorses in the barrage. I felt deranged for days afterward, as if I'd lived through the end of the world.

By the time I got home, though, I'd stopped thinking about that or any of the other horrific things we'd seen—casualties from an infantry assault through a minefield, starving civilians, MiG jets circling us, looking for a place to drop their bombs. I mentally buried all of it until one day a few months later when I went into the subway at rush hour to catch the C train downtown. Suddenly I found myself backed up against an iron support column, convinced I was going to die. For some reason everything seemed like a threat: there were too many people on the platform, the trains were moving too fast, the lights were too bright, the world was too loud. I couldn't really explain what was wrong, but I was more scared than I'd ever been in Afghanistan.

I stood there with my back to the column until I couldn't take it anymore, and then I sprinted for the exit and walked home. The nation wasn't at war yet, and I had no idea that what I'd just experienced had anything to do with combat; I just thought I was going crazy. For the next several months I kept having panic attacks whenever I was in a small place with too many people—airplanes, ski gondolas, bars. The incidents eventually stopped happening, and I didn't think about it again until two or three years later, when I found myself at a family picnic, talking to a woman who worked as a psychotherapist. The United States had just invaded Iraq, and that may have been what prompted her to ask whether I'd been traumatized by the wars I'd covered. I told her that I didn't think so, but that for a while I'd had panic attacks in crowded places. She nodded.

"That's called post-traumatic stress disorder," she said. "You'll be hearing a lot more about that in the next few years."

What I had was classic short-term PTSD. From an evolutionary perspective, it's exactly the response you want to have when your life is in danger: you want to be vigilant, you want to avoid situations where you are not in control, you want to react to strange noises, you want to sleep lightly and wake easily, you want to have flashbacks and nightmares that remind you of specific threats to your life, and you want to be, by turns, angry and depressed. Anger keeps you ready to fight, and depression keeps you from being too active and putting yourself in more danger. Flashbacks also serve to remind you of the danger that's out there—a "highly efficient single-event survival-learning mechanism," as one researcher termed it. All humans react to trauma in this way, and most mammals do as well. It may be unpleasant, but it's preferable to getting killed.

Like depression and grief, PTSD can be exacerbated by other factors but tends to diminish with time. My panic attacks eased up and eventually stopped, though a strange emotionality took their place. I found myself tearing up at things that I otherwise would have just smiled at or not noticed at all. Once, I got so emotional watching an elderly clerk doing her job at the post office that I had to walk out and come back later to send my mail. It happened in my sleep too: strange combat dreams that weren't scary but somehow triggered a catastrophic outpouring of sorrow. Invariably I would wake up and just lie there in the dark, trying to figure out why feelings that seemed to belong to other people kept spilling out of me. I wasn't a soldier—though I'd spent plenty of time with soldiers—and at that point I hadn't lost any close friends in combat. And yet when I went to sleep, it was like I became part of some larger human experience that was utterly heartbreaking. It was far too much to acknowledge when I was awake.

I had a much older friend named Joanna who was very concerned about how I was faring psychologically after the wars I'd covered. Joanna died soon after I came back from one particularly long stint overseas, and I had almost no reaction to the news until I started talking to her nephew about the trips she'd taken during the early 1960s to register black voters in the South. People were getting killed for doing that, and I remember Joanna telling me that she and her husband, Ellis, never knew if she would make it back alive when she left on those trips. After a year of covering combat there was something about her willingness to die for others—for human dignity—that completely undid me. Stories about soldiers had the same effect on me: completely divorced from any sense of patriotism, accounts of great bravery could emotionally annihilate me. The human concern for others would seem to be the one story that, adequately told, no person can fully bear to hear.

Joanna's husband, Ellis, was part Lakotah, part Apache, and had been born on a wagon in Missouri just before the Great Depression. He married Joanna when she was sixteen and he was twenty-five. I would go visit them on weekends when I was in college; Joanna would put me to work around their property until it got dark, and then the three of us would have dinner together. Afterward, Ellis and I would retreat to the living room to talk. He would smoke Carlton ultralights and drink cold coffee and tell me about the world, and I mostly just sat and listened. He seemed to have access to a kind of ancient human knowledge that completely transcended the odd, cloistered life that he was living in Connecticut when I met him. One of his favorite stories took place during some senseless war between the English and the French. At one point it was proposed that a lighthouse off the coast of France be destroyed by British warships to impede shipping and navigation.

"Sir," an English admiral reminded the king, "we are at war with the French, not with the entire human race."

If war were purely and absolutely bad in every single aspect and toxic in all its effects, it would probably not happen as often as it does. But in addition to all the destruction and loss of life, war also inspires ancient human virtues of courage, loyalty, and selflessness that can be utterly intoxicating to the people who experience them. Ellis's story is affecting because it demonstrates war's ability to ennoble people rather than just debase them. The Iroquois Nation presumably understood the transformative power of war when they developed parallel systems of government that protected civilians from warriors and vice versa. Peacetime leaders, called sachems, were often chosen by women and had complete authority over the civil affairs of the tribe until war broke out. At that point war leaders took over, and their sole concern was the physical survival of the tribe. They were not concerned with justice or harmony or fairness, they were concerned only with defeating the enemy. If the enemy tried to negotiate an end to hostilities, however, it was the sachems, not the war leaders, who made the final decision. If the offer was accepted, the war leaders stepped down so that the sachems could resume leadership of the tribe.

The Iroquois system reflected the radically divergent priorities that a society must have during peacetime and during war. Because modern society often fights wars far away from the civilian population, soldiers wind up being the only people who have to switch back and forth. Siegfried Sassoon, who was wounded in World War I, wrote a poem called "Sick Leave" that perfectly described the crippling alienation many soldiers feel at home: "In bitter safety I awake, unfriended," he wrote. "And while the dawn begins with slashing rain / I think of the Battalion in the mud."

Given the profound alienation of modern society, when combat vets say that they miss the war, they might be having an entirely healthy response to life back home. Iroquois warriors did not have to struggle with that sort of alienation because warfare and society existed in such close proximity that there was effectively no transition from one to the other. In addition, defeat meant that a catastrophic violence might be visited upon everyone they loved, and in that context, fighting to the death made complete sense from both an evolutionary and an emotional point of view. Certainly, some Iroquois warriors must have been traumatized by the warfare they were engaged in—much of it was conducted at close quarters with clubs and hatchets—but they didn't have to contain that trauma within themselves. The entire society was undergoing wartime trauma, so it was a collective experience—and therefore an easier one.

A rapid recovery from psychological trauma must have been exceedingly important in our evolutionary past, and individuals who could climb out of their shock reaction and resume fleeing or fighting must have survived at higher rates than those who couldn't. A 2011 study of street children in Burundi found the lowest PTSD rates among the *most* aggressive and violent children. Aggression seemed to buffer them from the effects of previous trauma that they had experienced. Because trauma recovery is greatly affected by social factors, and because it presumably had such high survival value in our evolutionary past, one way to evaluate the health of a society might be to look at how quickly its soldiers or warriors recover, psychologically, from the experience of combat.

Almost everyone exposed to trauma reacts by having some sort of short-term reaction to it—acute PTSD. That reaction clearly has evolved in mammals to keep them both reactive to danger and out of harm's way until the threat has passed. Long-term PTSD, on the other hand—the kind that can last years or even a lifetime—is clearly maladaptive and relatively uncommon. Many studies have shown that in the general population, at most 20 percent of people who have been traumatized get long-term PTSD. Rather than being better prepared for extraordinary danger, these people become poorly adjusted to everyday life. Rape is one of the most psychologically devastating things that can happen to a person, for example—far more traumatizing than most military deployments—and according to a 1992 study, close to one hundred percent of rape survivors exhibited extreme trauma immediately afterward. And yet almost half of rape survivors experienced a significant decline in their trauma symptoms within weeks or months of their assault.

That is a far faster recovery rate than soldiers have

exhibited in the recent wars America has fought. One of the reasons, paradoxically, is because the trauma of combat is interwoven with other, positive experiences that become difficult to separate from the harm. "Treating combat veterans is different from treating rape victims, because rape victims don't have this idea that some aspects of their experience are worth retaining," I was told by Dr. Rachel Yehuda, the director of traumatic stress studies at Mount Sinai Hospital in New York. Yehuda has studied PTSD in a wide range of people, including combat veterans and Holocaust survivors. "For most people in combat, their experiences range from the best of times to the worst of times. It's the most important thing someone has ever done—especially since these people are so young when they go in—and it's probably the first time they've ever been free, completely, of societal constraints. They're going to miss being entrenched in this defining world."

Except for sociopaths, one of the most traumatic events that a soldier can experience is witnessing harm to others—even to the enemy. In a survey carried out after the first Gulf War by David Marlowe, an anthropologist who later worked for the US Department of Defense, combat veterans reported that killing an enemy soldier, or even witnessing one getting killed, was more distressing than being wounded themselves. But the very worst experience, by far, was having a friend die. In war after war, army after army, losing a buddy is considered the most devastating thing that can possibly happen. It is far more disturbing than experiencing mortal danger oneself and often serves as a trigger for psychological breakdown on the battlefield or later in life.

Still, most soldiers go through that and other terrible experiences and don't wind up with long-term trauma. Multiple studies, including a 2007 analysis from the Institute of Medicine and the National Research Council, found that a person's chance of getting chronic PTSD is in great part a function of their experiences *before* going to war. Statistically, the 20 percent of people who fail to overcome trauma tend to be those who are already burdened by psychological issues, either because they inherited them or because they suffered abuse as children. If you fought in Vietnam and your twin brother did not—but he suffers from a psychiatric disorder such as schizophrenia— you are statistically more likely to get PTSD. If you experienced the death of a loved one, or if you weren't held enough as a child, you are up to seven times more likely to develop the kinds of anxiety disorders that contribute to PTSD. According to a 2000 study in the *Journal of Consulting and Clinical Psychology*, if you have an educational deficit, if you are female, if you have a low IQ, or if you were abused as a child, you are also at an elevated risk of developing PTSD. (The elevated risk for women is due to their greater likelihood of getting PTSD after a physical assault. For other forms of trauma, men and women are fairly equal.) These risk factors are nearly as predictive of PTSD as the severity of the trauma itself.

Suicide is often seen as an extreme expression of PTSD, but researchers have not yet found any relationship between suicide and combat. Combat veterans are, statistically, no more likely to kill themselves than veterans who were never under fire. The much-discussed estimate of twenty-two vets a day committing suicide in the United States is deceptive: it was only in 2008 that—for the first time in decades—the suicide rate among veterans surpassed the civilian rate in America, and though each death is enormously tragic, the majority of those veterans were over the age of fifty. Many were Vietnam vets and, generally speaking, the more time that passes after a trauma, the less likely a suicide is to have anything to do with it. Among younger vets, deployment to Iraq or Afghanistan actually *lowers* the risk of suicide, because soldiers with obvious mental health issues are not deployed with their units.

Further confusing the issue, voluntary service has resulted in a military population that has a disproportionate number of young people with a history of sexual abuse. One theory for this holds that military service is an easy way for young people to get out of their home, and so the military will disproportionally draw recruits from troubled families. According to a 2014 study in the American Medical Association's *JAMA Psychiatry*, men with military service are now twice as likely to report sexual assault during their childhood as men who never served. This was not true during the draft. Sexual abuse is a well-known predictor of depression and other mental health issues, and the military suicide rate may in part be a result of that.

Killing seems to traumatize people regardless of the danger they're in or the perceived righteousness of their cause. Pilots of unmanned drones, who watch their missiles kill human beings by remote camera, have been calculated to have the same PTSD rates as pilots who fly actual combat missions in war zones. And even among regular infantry, danger and trauma are not necessarily connected. During the 1973 Yom Kippur War, when Israel was simultaneously invaded by Egypt and Syria, rear-base troops had psychological breakdowns at three times the rate of elite frontline troops, relative to the casualties they suffered. (In other words, rear-base troops had fairly light casualties but suffered a disproportionately high level of psychiatric breakdowns.) Similarly, more than 80 percent of psychiatric casualties in the US Army's VII Corps came from support units that took almost no incoming fire during the air campaign of the first Gulf War.

The discrepancy might be due to the fact that intensive training and danger create what is known as unit cohesion—strong emotional bonds within the company or the platoon—and high unit cohesion is correlated with lower rates of psychiatric breakdown. During World War II, American airborne units had some of the lowest psychiatric casualty rates of the entire US military, relative to their number of wounded. The same is true for armies in other countries: Sri Lankan special forces experience far more combat than line troops, and yet in 2010 they were found to suffer from significantly lower rates of both physical and mental health issues. (The one mental health issue they led everyone else in was "hazardous drinking.") And Israeli commanders suffered four times the mortality rate of their men during the Yom Kippur War, yet had one-fifth the rate of psychological breakdown on the battlefield.

All this is a new way to think about battlefield trauma, however. For most of America's history, psychological breakdown on the battlefield, as well as impairment afterward, has been written off to neuroses, shell shock, or simple cowardice. When men have failed to obey orders due to trauma, they have been beaten, imprisoned, "treated" with electrocution, or simply shot as a warning to others. It was not until after the Vietnam War that the American Psychiatric Association (APA) listed combat trauma as an official diagnosis. Tens of thousands of vets were struggling with "post-Vietnam syndrome"—nightmares, insomnia, addiction, paranoia—and their struggle could no longer be written off to weakness or personal failings. Obviously, these problems could also affect war reporters, cops, firemen, or anyone else subjected to trauma. In 1980, the APA finally included post-traumatic stress disorder in the third edition of the *Diagnostic and Statistical Manual of Mental Disorders*.

Thirty-five years after finally acknowledging the problem, the US military now has the highest reported PTSD rate in its history—and probably in the world. American soldiers appear to suffer PTSD at around twice the rate of British soldiers who were in combat with them. The United States currently spends more than $4 billion annually in disability compensation for PTSD, most of which will continue for the entire lifetime of these veterans. Horrific experiences are unfortunately a human universal, but long-term impairment from them is not, and despite billions of dollars spent on treatment, roughly half of Iraq and Afghanistan veterans have applied for permanent PTSD disability. Since only 10 percent of our armed forces experience actual combat, the majority of vets claiming to suffer from PTSD seem to have been affected by something other than direct exposure to danger.

This is not a new phenomenon: decade after decade and war after war, American combat deaths have generally dropped while disability claims have risen. Most disability claims are for medical issues and should decline with casualty rates and combat intensity, but they don't. They are in an almost inverse relationship with one another. Soldiers in Vietnam suffered one-quarter the mortality rate of troops in World War II, for example, but filed for both physical and psychological disability compensation at a rate that was 50 percent higher. It's tempting to attribute that to the toxic reception they had at home, but that doesn't seem to be the case. Today's vets claim three times the number of disabilities that Vietnam vets did, despite a generally warm reception back home and a casualty rate that, thank God, is roughly one-third what it was in Vietnam. Today, most disability claims are for hearing loss, tinnitus, and PTSD—the latter two of which can be imagined, exaggerated, or even faked.

Part of the problem is bureaucratic: in an effort to speed up access to benefits, in 2010 the Veterans Administration declared that soldiers no longer have to cite a specific incident—a firefight, a roadside bomb—in order to be eligible for disability compensation. They simply had to claim "a credible fear of being attacked" during deployment. As with welfare and other so-called "entitlement" programs, a less rigorous definition of need—though well-intentioned—may have produced a system that is vulnerable to error or fraud. Self-reporting of PTSD by veterans has been found to lead to a misdiagnosis rate as high as 50 percent. A recent investigation by the VA Office of Inspector General found that the higher a veteran's PTSD disability rating, the more treatment he or she tends to seek until achieving a rating of 100 percent, at which point treatment visits plummet and many vets quit completely. (A 100 percent disability rating entitles a veteran to a tax-free income of around $3,000 a month.) In theory, the most traumatized people should be seeking *more* help, not less. Investigators reluctantly came to the conclusion that some vets were getting treatment simply to raise their disability rating and claim more compensation.

In addition to being an enormous waste of taxpayer money, misdiagnosis does real harm to vets who truly need help. One Veterans Administration counselor I spoke with, who asked to remain anonymous, described having to physically protect someone in a PTSD support group because other vets wanted to beat him up for seeming to fake his trauma. This counselor said that many combat veterans actively avoid the VA because they worry about losing their temper around patients who they think are milking the system. "It's the real deals—the guys who have seen the most—that this tends to bother," he told me.

The vast majority of traumatized vets are *not* faking their symptoms, however. They return from wars that are safer than those their fathers and grandfathers fought, and yet far greater numbers of them wind up alienated and depressed. This is true *even for people who didn't experience combat*. In other words, the problem doesn't seem to be trauma on the battlefield so much as reentry into society. And vets are not alone in this. It's common knowledge in the Peace Corps that as stressful as life in a developing country can be, returning to a modern country can be far harder. One study found that one in four Peace Corps volunteers reported experiencing significant depression after their return home, and that figure more than doubled for people who had been evacuated from their host country during wartime or some other kind of emergency.

Studies from around the world show that recovery from war—from any trauma—is heavily influenced by the society one belongs to, and there are societies that make that process relatively easy. Modern society does not seem to be one of them. Among American vets, if one weeds out obviously exaggerated trauma on the one hand and deep trauma on the other, there are still enormous numbers of people who had utterly ordinary wartime experiences and yet feel dangerously alienated back home. Clinically speaking, such alienation is not the same as PTSD— and maybe deserves its own diagnostic term—but both result from military service abroad, so it's understandable that vets and clinicians alike are prone to conflating them. Either way, it makes one wonder exactly what it is about modern society that is so mortally dispiriting to come home to.

Any discussion of veterans and their common experience of alienation must address the fact that so many soldiers find themselves missing the war after it's over. That troubling fact can be found in written accounts from war after war, country after country, century after century. As awkward as it is to say, part of the trauma of war seems to be giving it up. "For the first time in [our] lives . . . we were in a tribal sort of situation where we could help each other without fear," a former gunner in the 62nd Coast Artillery named Win Stracke told oral historian Studs Terkel for his book *The Good War*. (Stracke was also a well-known folk singer and labor organizer who was blacklisted during the McCarthy era for his political activity.) "There were fifteen men to a gun. You had fifteen guys who for the first time in their lives were not living in a competitive society. We had no hopes of becoming officers. I liked that feeling very much ... It was the absence of competition and boundaries and all those phony standards that created the thing I loved about the Army."

Adversity often leads people to depend more on one another, and that closeness can produce a kind of nostalgia for the hard times that even civilians are susceptible to. After World War II, many Londoners claimed to miss the exciting and perilous days of the Blitz ("I wouldn't mind having an evening like it, say, once a week—ordinarily there's no excitement," one man commented to Mass-Observation about the air raids), and the war that is missed doesn't even have to be a shooting war: "I am a survivor of the AIDS epidemic," an American man wrote in 2014 on the comment board of an online lecture about war. "Now that AIDS is no longer a death sentence, I must admit that I miss those days of extreme brotherhood ... which led to deep emotions and understandings that are above anything I have felt since the plague years."

What people miss presumably isn't danger or loss but the unity that these things often engender. There are obvious stresses on a person in a group, but there may be even greater stresses on a person in isolation, so during disasters there is a net gain in well-being. Most primates, including humans, are intensely social, and there are very few instances of lone primates surviving in the wild. A modern soldier returning from combat—or a survivor of Sarajevo—goes from the kind of close-knit group that humans evolved for, back into a society where most people work outside the home, children are educated by strangers, families are isolated from wider communities, and personal gain almost completely eclipses collective good. Even if he or she is part of a family, that is not the same as belonging to a group that shares resources and experiences almost everything collectively. Whatever the technological advances of modern society— and they're nearly miraculous—the individualized lifestyles that those technologies spawn seem to be deeply brutalizing to the human spirit.

"You'll have to be prepared to say that we are not a good society—that we are an *antihuman* society," anthropologist Sharon Abramowitz warned when I tried this idea out on her. Abramowitz was in Ivory Coast as a Peace Corps volunteer during the start of the civil war in 2002 and experienced firsthand the extremely close bonds created by hardship and danger. "We are not good to each other. Our tribalism is to an extremely narrow group of people: our children, our spouse, maybe our parents. Our society is alienating, technical, cold, and mystifying. Our fundamental desire, as human beings, is to be close to others, and our society does not allow for that."

One of the most noticeable things about life in the military, even in support units, is that you are almost never alone. Day after day, month after month, you are close enough to speak to, if not touch, a dozen or more people. When I was with American soldiers at a remote outpost in Afghanistan, we slept ten to a hut in bunks that were only a few feet apart. I could touch three other men with my outstretched hand from where I lay. They snored, they talked, they got up in the middle of the night to use the piss tubes, but we always felt safe because we were in a group. The outpost was attacked dozens of times, yet I slept better surrounded by those noisy, snoring men than I ever did camping alone in the woods of New England.

That kind of group sleeping has been the norm throughout human history and is still commonplace in most of the world. Northern European societies are among the few where people sleep alone or with

a partner in a private room, and that may have significant implications for mental health in general and
for PTSD in particular. Virtually all mammals seem
to benefit from companionship; even lab rats recover
more quickly from trauma if they are caged with
other rats rather than alone. In humans, lack of social
support has been found to be twice as reliable at predicting PTSD as the severity of the trauma itself. In
other words, you could be mildly traumatized—on a
par with, say, an ordinary rear-base deployment to
Afghanistan—and experience long-term PTSD simply because of a lack of social support back home.

Anthropologist Brandon Kohrt found a similar
phenomenon in the villages of southern Nepal, where
a civil war has been rumbling for years. There are
two kinds of villages in that area: exclusively Hindu
ones that have sharp class distinctions, and mixed
Hindu and Buddhist ones that are far more open and
cohesive. Child soldiers of either sex who went back
to stratified villages could remain traumatized almost
indefinitely, while those who returned to more communal villages tended to recover fairly quickly.
"Some had trauma rates that were no different from
children that had not gone to war at all," Kohrt told
me about those ex-combatants. "PTSD is a disorder of

95

recovery, and if treatment only focuses on identifying symptoms, it pathologizes and alienates vets. But if the focus is on family and community, it puts them in a situation of collective healing."

Israel is arguably the only modern country that retains a sufficient sense of community to mitigate the effects of combat on a mass scale. Despite decades of intermittent war, the Israel Defense Forces have by some measures a PTSD rate as low as 1 percent. Two of the foremost reasons may have to do with the proximity of the combat—the war is virtually on their doorstep—and national military service. "Being in the military is something that most people have done," I was told by Dr. Arieh Shalev, who has devoted the last twenty years to studying PTSD. "Those who come back from combat are reintegrated into a society where those experiences are very well understood. We did a study of seventeen-year-olds who had lost their father in the military, compared to those who had lost their fathers to accidents. The ones whose fathers died in combat did much better than those whose fathers hadn't."

According to Shalev, the closer the public is to the actual combat, the better the war will be understood and the less difficulty soldiers will have when they come home. During the Yom Kippur War of 1973, many Israeli soldiers were fighting on the Golan Heights with their homes at their backs. Of the 1,323 soldiers who were wounded in that war and referred for psychiatric evaluation, only around 20 percent were diagnosed with PTSD, and less than 2 percent retained that diagnosis three decades later. The Israelis are benefiting from what the author and ethicist Austin Dacey describes as a "shared public meaning" of the war. Shared public meaning gives soldiers a context for their losses and their sacrifice that is acknowledged by most of the society. That helps keep at bay the sense of futility and rage that can develop among soldiers during a war that doesn't seem to end.

Such public meaning is probably not generated by the kinds of formulaic phrases, such as "Thank you for your service," that many Americans now feel compelled to offer soldiers and vets. Neither is it generated by honoring vets at sporting events, allowing them to board planes first, or giving them minor discounts at stores. If anything, these token acts only deepen the chasm between the military and civilian populations by highlighting the fact that some people serve their country but the vast majority don't. In

Israel, where around half of the population serves in the military, reflexively thanking someone for their service makes as little sense as thanking them for paying their taxes. It doesn't cross anyone's mind.

Because modern society has almost completely eliminated trauma and violence from everyday life, anyone who *does* suffer those things is deemed to be extraordinarily unfortunate. This gives people access to sympathy and resources but also creates an identity of victimhood that can delay recovery. Anthropologist Danny Hoffman, who studied Mende tribal combatants both during and after civil wars in Liberia and Sierra Leone, found that international relief organizations introduced the idea of victimhood to combatants who until then had rarely, if ever, thought of themselves in those terms. "The language of 'I am a victim too' did not originate from the combatants themselves," Hoffman told me. "[Aid organizations] would come in and say, 'This is how you're supposed to be feeling ... and if you do, then you'll have access to food supplies and training.'"

In such a poor society, food donations and job training gave an enormous advantage to ex-combatants.

The consequence, Hoffman told me, was that ex-combatants were incentivized to see themselves as victims rather than as perpetrators. These people committed terrible acts of violence during their wars, and many of them felt enormously guilty about it, but they were never able to work through those feelings because their victim status eclipsed more accurate and meaningful understandings of violence. Mende combatants often described combat as something that makes the heart "heat up," transforming a fighter to the point where he is thought to have literally become someone else. In that state he is capable of both great courage and great cruelty. Such a state of hyper-arousal is familiar to many soldiers or athletes and has a firm basis in the neurobiology of the brain. For the Mende, it means that the moral excesses of the battle-field don't necessarily have to be brought home.

I was in both Liberia and Sierra Leone during those wars, and the combatants who had a "hot heart" were unmistakable. They wore amulets and magical charms and acted as if they were possessed, deliberately running into gunfire and dancing while firing their weapons to prove how brave they were. Other people's lives didn't seem to matter to them because their *own* lives didn't seem to matter to them.

They were true nihilists, and that made them the most terrifying human beings I've ever encountered. According to Hoffman, even highly traumatized ex-combatants such as these could have been reincorporated into Mende society if indigenous concepts like the "hot heart" had been applied. Their classification as victims, however—with the attendant perks and benefits common to Western society—made their reintegration much harder.

The civil war in nearby Ivory Coast unfolded in much the same way, although relief organizations had less access to combatants afterward. "In tribal cultures, combat can be part of the maturation process," I was told by Sharon Abramowitz, who was in Ivory Coast with the Peace Corps in 2002. "When youth return from combat, their return is seen as integral to their own society—they don't feel like outsiders. In the United States we valorize our vets with words and posters and signs, but we don't give them what's really important to Americans, what really sets you apart as someone who is valuable to society—we don't give them jobs. All the praise in the world doesn't mean anything if you're not recognized by society as someone who can contribute valuable labor."

IN BITTER SAFETY I AWAKE

Anthropologists like Kohrt, Hoffman, and Abramo-witz have identified three factors that seem to crucially affect a combatant's transition back into civilian life. The United States seems to rank low on all three. First, cohesive and egalitarian tribal societies do a very good job at mitigating the effects of trauma, but by their very nature, many modern societies are exactly the opposite: hierarchical and alienating. America's great wealth, although a blessing in many ways, has allowed for the growth of an individualistic society that suffers high rates of depression and anxiety. Both are correlated with chronic PTSD.

Secondly, ex-combatants shouldn't be seen—or be encouraged to see themselves—as victims. One can be deeply traumatized, as firemen are by the deaths of both colleagues and civilians, without being viewed through the lens of victimhood. Lifelong disability payments for a disorder like PTSD, which is both treatable and usually not chronic, risks turning veterans into a victim class that is entirely dependent on the government for their livelihood. The United States is a wealthy country that may be able to afford this, but in human terms, the veterans can't. The one way that soldiers are never allowed to see themselves during deployment is as victims, because the passivity of victimhood can get them killed. It's yelled, beaten, and drilled out of them long before they get close to the battlefield. But when they come home they find themselves being viewed so sympathetically that they're often excused from having to fully function in society. Some of them truly can't function, and those people should be taken care of immediately; but imagine how confusing it must be to the rest of them.

Perhaps most important, veterans need to feel that they're just as necessary and productive back in society as they were on the battlefield. Iroquois warriors who dominated just about every tribe within 500 miles of their home territory would return to a community that still needed them to hunt and fish and participate in the fabric of everyday life. There was no transition when they came home because—much like in Israel—the battlefield was an extension of society, and vice versa. Recent studies of something called "social resilience" have identified resource sharing and egalitarian wealth distribution as major components of a society's ability to recover from hardship. And societies that rank high on social resilience—such as kibbutz settlements in Israel—provide soldiers with a significantly stronger buffer against PTSD than low-resilience societies. In fact, social resilience is an even better predictor of trauma recovery than the level of resilience of the person himself.

Unfortunately, for the past decade American soldiers have returned to a country that displays many indicators of low social resilience. Resources are not shared equally, a quarter of children live in poverty, jobs are hard to get, and minimum wage is almost impossible to live on. Instead of being able to work and contribute to society—a highly therapeutic thing to do—a large percentage of veterans are just offered lifelong disability payments. And they accept, of course—why shouldn't they? A society that doesn't distinguish between degrees of trauma can't expect its warriors to, either.

CALLING HOME FROM MARS

BECAUSE MY FATHER GREW UP IN EUROPE, I WENT there a lot when I was young, first with my family and then on my own. In my early twenties I wound up in Pamplona, Spain, for the festival of San Fermin, the infamous running of the bulls. One night I found myself in a small bar with sawdust on the floor talking to two young Spaniards who were so drunk they could barely stand up. One wore a white T-shirt and was drinking red wine out of a leather bota. Every time he squirted wine into his mouth, most of it went all over his shirt. He was also wearing a plastic Viking helmet with fake gemstones around the rim that he seemed to have completely forgotten about, though it was impossible to ignore if you were talking to him. He was drinking and grinning like a fool and had his arm around his buddy, and everything was going fine until three Moroccan guys walked into the bar. They were as drunk and happy as everyone else until the biggest one spotted the Viking helmet on my friend's head. He strode right up and grabbed it. "That helmet's mine!" he shouted in French. "You stole it!"

I translated because I was the only person who spoke both French and Spanish. My friend managed to get his hands on the helmet and shouted, "That's not true, the helmet's mine!" And so it began. Suddenly all five men had their hands on the helmet; they weren't throwing punches because no one wanted to let go, but it was clearly headed that way. The men lurched around the room grunting in two languages and gradually deforming the helmet until my friend yelled, "*Para! Para! Para!*" and everyone stopped. "It's starting to rip!" my friend said, pointing to the helmet.

They were destroying the thing they all wanted, but no one would let go. It got very quiet. They all stared at each other. Finally my friend turned to me and asked, in his most elegant and formulaic Spanish, if I would take his place at the helmet and defend it with the full honor of my family and my name. I was still calculating how long you have to know someone before you have to back them up in a bar fight—hours? Minutes?—but I told him that I would. My friend withdrew his hand from the helmet and replaced it with mine. Now I was in the ring facing three drunk Moroccans, and my friend was over at the bar conferring with the bartender. It had all the hushed formality of a sidebar conference at a criminal trial.

After a moment the bartender straightened up and pulled a screw-top jug of red wine out from under the bar and handed it to my friend. Complete silence now, and a kind of theatrical slowness to things, as if we were all acting roles that had been scripted long ago. My friend approached the absurd little circle and filled the helmet with red wine. I remember it reaching my fingertips and staining them red. Then with great fanfare the Spaniard placed one hand under the helmet and told everyone to let go. We all looked at each other and one by one released our grip. Now my friend stood with the helmet in his upturned hand, red wine slopping over the brim. He turned and addressed the most aggressive of his adversaries: "You are a guest in my country," he said, as I translated. "So you drink first."

He offered the helmet to the Moroccan, who accepted it and drank from the brim, wine running down his neck, and then passed it to his left. Each man drank and passed the helmet clockwise, and when it came to me, I did the same. The helmet went around and around, and when it was empty it got filled up with more red wine. The other patrons started to go back to their drinking and their conversations, and eventually the former combatants skipped the helmet and started passing around the jug itself. Pretty soon the jug was empty and another one was sent for, and that was passed around as well. I got drawn into other conversations and an hour or so later I looked over to see all five men standing in a line with their arms around each other, singing songs in their two languages. The helmet was forgotten under a table at their feet.

What I liked about the encounter was that it showed how very close the energy of male conflict and male closeness can be. It's almost as if they are two facets of the same quality; just change a few details and instead of heading toward collision, the men head toward unity. There seemed to be a great human potential out there, organized around the idea of belonging, and the trick was to convince people that their interests had more in common than they had in conflict. I once asked a combat vet if he'd rather have an enemy in his life or another close friend. He looked at me like I was crazy.

"Oh, an enemy, a hundred percent," he said. "Not even close. I already got a lot of friends." He thought about it a little longer. "Anyway, all my best friends I've gotten into fights with—knock-down, drag-out fights. Granted we were always drunk when it happened, but think about that."

He shook his head as if even he couldn't believe it.

There's no use arguing that modern society isn't a kind of paradise. The vast majority of us don't, personally, have to grow or kill our own food, build our own dwellings, or defend ourselves from wild animals and enemies. In one day we can travel a thousand miles by pushing our foot down on a gas pedal or around the world by booking a seat on an airplane. When we are in pain we have narcotics that dull it out of existence, and when we are depressed we have pills that change the chemistry of our brains. We understand an enormous amount about the universe, from subatomic particles to our own bodies to galaxy clusters, and we use that knowledge to make life even better and easier for ourselves. The poorest people in modern society enjoy a level of physical comfort that was unimaginable a thousand years ago, and the wealthiest people literally live the way gods were imagined to have.

And yet.

There are many costs to modern society, starting with its toll on the global ecosystem and working one's way down to its toll on the human psyche, but the most dangerous loss may be to community. If the human race is under threat in some way that we don't yet understand, it will probably be at a community level that we either solve the problem or fail to. If the future of the planet depends on, say, rationing water, communities of neighbors will be able to enforce new rules far more effectively than even local government. It's how we evolved to exist, and it obviously works.

Two of the behaviors that set early humans apart were the systematic sharing of food and altruistic group defense. Other primates did very little of either but, increasingly, hominids did, and those behaviors helped set them on an evolutionary path that produced the modern world. The earliest and most basic definition of community—of tribe—would be the group of people that you would both help feed and help defend. A society that doesn't offer its members the chance to act selflessly in these ways isn't a society in any tribal sense of the word; it's just a political entity that, lacking enemies, will probably fall apart on its own. Soldiers experience this tribal way of thinking at war, but when they come home they realize that the tribe they were actually fighting for wasn't their country, it was their unit. It makes absolutely no sense to make sacrifices for a group that, itself, isn't willing to make sacrifices for you. That is the position American soldiers have been in for the past decade and a half.

There was a period during the run-up to the Iraq War in 2003 when a bumper sticker that read NO BLOOD FOR OIL started appearing on American cars. Implicit in the slogan was the assumption that the Iraq War was over oil, but the central irony of putting such a message on a machine *that runs on oil* seemed lost on most people. There is virtually no source of oil that does not incur enormous damage to either the local population or the environment, and driving a car means that you're unavoidably contributing to that damage. I was deeply opposed to the Iraq War for other reasons. But the antiwar rhetoric around the topic of oil by people who continued to use it to fuel their cars betrayed a larger hypocrisy that extended across the political spectrum. The public is often accused of being disconnected from its military, but frankly it's disconnected from just about everything. Farming, mineral extraction, gas and oil production, bulk cargo transport, logging, fishing, infrastructure construction—all the industries that keep the nation going are mostly unacknowledged by the people who depend on them most.

As great a sacrifice as soldiers make, American workers arguably make a greater one. Far more Americans lose their lives every year doing dangerous jobs than died *during the entire Afghan War*. In 2014, for example, 4,679 workers lost their lives on the job. More than 90 percent of those deaths were of young men working in industries that have a mortality rate equivalent to most units in the US military. Jobs that are directly observable to the public, like construction, tend to be less respected and less well paid than jobs that happen behind closed doors, like real estate or finance. And yet it is exactly these jobs that provide society's immediate physical needs. Construction workers are more important to everyday life than stockbrokers and yet are far lower down the social and financial ladder.

This fundamental lack of connectedness allows people to act in trivial but incredibly selfish ways. Rachel Yehuda pointed to littering as the perfect example of an everyday symbol of disunity in society. "It's a horrible thing to see because it sort of encapsulates this idea that you're in it alone, that there isn't a shared ethos of trying to protect something shared," she told me. "It's the embodiment of every man for himself. It's the opposite of the military."

In this sense, littering is an exceedingly petty version of claiming a billion-dollar bank bailout or fraudulently claiming disability payments. When you throw trash on the ground, you apparently don't see yourself as truly belonging to the world that you're walking around in. And when you fraudulently claim money from the government, you are ultimately stealing from your friends, family, and neighbors—or somebody else's friends, family, and neighbors. That diminishes you morally far more than it diminishes your country financially. My friend Ellis was once asked by a troubled young boy whether there was any compelling reason for him not to pull the legs off a spider. Ellis said that there was.

"Well, spiders don't feel any pain," the boy retorted.

"It's not the spider I'm worried about," Ellis said.

The ultimate act of disaffiliation isn't littering or fraud, of course, but violence against your own people. When the Navajo Nation—the *Diné*, in their language—were rounded up and confined to a reservation in the 1860s, a terrifying phenomenon became more prominent in their culture. The warrior skills that had protected the *Diné* for thousands of years were no longer relevant in this dismal new era, and people worried that those same skills would now be turned inward, against society. That strengthened their belief in what were known as skinwalkers, or *yee naaldlooshii*.

Skinwalkers were almost always male and wore the pelt of a sacred animal so that they could subvert that animal's powers to kill people in the community. They could travel impossibly fast across the desert and their eyes glowed like coals and they could supposedly paralyze you with a single look. They were thought to attack remote homesteads at night and kill people and sometimes eat their bodies. People were still scared of skinwalkers when I lived on the Navajo Reservation in 1983, and frankly, by the time I left, I was too.

Virtually every culture in the world has its version of the skinwalker myth. In Europe, for example, they are called werewolves (literally "man-wolf" in Old English). The myth addresses a fundamental fear in human society: that you can defend against external enemies but still remain vulnerable to one lone madman in your midst. Anglo-American culture doesn't recognize the skinwalker threat but has its own version. Starting in the early 1980s, the frequency of rampage shootings in the United States began to rise more and more rapidly until it doubled around 2006. Rampages are usually defined as attacks where people are randomly targeted and four or more are killed in one place, usually shot to death by a lone gunman. As such, those crimes conform almost exactly to the kind of threat that the Navajo seemed most to fear on the reservation: murder and mayhem committed by an individual who has rejected all social bonds and attacks people at their most vulnerable and unprepared. For modern society, that would mean not in their log hogans but in movie theaters, schools, shopping malls, places of worship, or simply walking down the street.

Seen in that light, it's revealing to look at the kinds of communities where those crimes usually occur. A rampage shooting has never happened in an urban ghetto, for example; in fact, indiscriminate attacks at schools almost always occur in otherwise safe, predominantly white towns. Around half of rampage killings happen in affluent or upper-middle-class communities, and the rest tend to happen in rural towns that are majority-white, Christian, and low-crime. Nearly 600 people have been killed by rampage shooters since the 1980s. Almost by definition, rampage killers are deeply disturbed sociopaths, but that just begs the question why sociopaths in high-crime urban neighborhoods don't turn their guns on other people the way they do in more affluent communities.

Gang shootings—as indiscriminate as they often are—still don't have the nihilistic intent of rampages. Rather, they are rooted in an exceedingly strong sense of group loyalty and revenge, and bystanders sometimes get killed in the process. The first time that the United States suffered a wave of rampage shootings was during the 1930s, when society had been severely stressed and fractured by the Great Depression. Profoundly disturbed, violent individuals might not have felt inhibited by the social bonds

that restrained previous generations of potential killers. Rampage killings dropped significantly during
World War II, then rose again in the 1980s and have
been rising ever since. It may be worth considering
whether middle-class American life—for all its material good fortune—has lost some essential sense of
unity that might otherwise discourage alienated men
from turning apocalyptically violent.

The last time the United States experienced that
kind of unity was—briefly—after the terrorist
attacks of September 11. There were no rampage
shootings for the next two years. The effect was
particularly pronounced in New York City, where
rates of violent crime, suicide, and psychiatric dis-
turbances dropped immediately. In many countries,
antisocial behavior is known to decline during wartime. New York's suicide rate dropped by around 20
percent in the six months following the attacks, the
murder rate dropped by 40 percent, and pharmacists
saw no increase in the number of first-time patients
filling prescriptions for antianxiety and antidepres-
sant medication. Furthermore, veterans who were
being treated for PTSD at the VA experienced a significant *drop* in their symptoms in the months after
the September 11 attacks.

One way to determine what is missing in day-to-day American life may be to examine what behaviors spontaneously arise when that life is disrupted.

I talked to my mom only one time from Mars," a Vietnam vet named Gregory Gomez told me about the physical and spiritual distance between his home and the war zone. Gomez is an Apache Indian who grew up in West Texas. Gomez says his grandfather was arrested and executed by Texas Rangers in 1915 because they wanted his land; they strung him from a tree limb, cut his genitals off, and stuffed them in his mouth. Consequently, Gomez says he felt no allegiance to the US government, but he volunteered for service in Vietnam anyway.

"Most of us Indian guys who went to Vietnam went because we were warriors," Gomez told me. "I did not fight for this country. I fought for Mother Earth. I wanted to experience combat. I wanted to see how I'd do."

Gomez was in a Marine Force Recon unit, one of the most elite designations in the US military. He was part of a four-man team that would insert by helicopter into the jungle north of the DMZ for weeks at a time. They had no medic and no air support, and Gomez said that they didn't dare eat C rations because they were afraid their body odor would give them away at close quarters. They ate Vietnamese food and watched enemy soldiers pass just yards away in the dense jungle. "Everyone who has lived through something like that has lived through trauma, and you can never go back," he told me. "You are seventeen or eighteen or nineteen and you just hit that wall. You become very old men."

American Indians, proportionally, provide more soldiers to America's wars than any other demographic group in the country. They are also the product of an ancient culture of warfare that takes great pains to protect the warrior from society, and vice versa. Although those traditions have obviously broken down since the end of the Indian Wars, there may be something to be learned from the principles upon which they stand. When Gomez came home to West Texas he essentially went into hiding for more than a decade. He didn't drink and he lived a normal life, except that occasionally he'd go to the corner store to get a soda and would wind up in Oklahoma City or East Texas without any idea how he got there. He finally started seeing a therapist at the VA as well as undergoing traditional Indian rituals. It was a combination that seemed to work: "We do a lot of sweat lodge ceremonies as part of a cleaning and purification," he told me. "The vision quest ceremony is normally a four-day ceremony, and you do fasting so your system is pretty cleaned out. You're detoxified, as it were. You're pretty high."

In the 1980s Gomez underwent an extremely painful ceremony called the Sun Dance—a traditional Lakotah ceremony that was banned for many years by the US government. It was finally made legal again in 1934. At the start of the ceremony, dancers have wooden skewers driven through the skin of their chests. Leather thongs are tied to the skewers and then attached to a tall pole at the center of the dance ground. To a steady drumbeat, the dancers shuffle in a circle and lean back on the thongs until, after many hours, the skewers finally tear free.

"I dance back and I throw my arms and yell and I can see the ropes and the piercing sticks like in slow motion, flying from my chest towards the grandfather tree," Gomez told me about the experience. "And I had this incredible feeling of euphoria and strength, like I could do anything. That's when the healing takes place. That's when life changes take place."

American tribes varied widely in their cultures and economies and so had different relationships to war. The nomadic horse cultures of the Northern Plains, such as the Lakotah and the Cheyenne, considered war to be a chance for young men to prove their honor and courage. The Apache avoided face-to-face combat in favor of raiding expeditions that relied on stealth and endurance. The sedentary Papago, whose economy was based largely on agriculture, considered war to be a form of insanity. Men who were forced into combat by attacks from other tribes had to undergo a sixteen-day purification ritual before they could reenter society. The entire community participated in these rituals because every person in the tribe was assumed to have been affected by the war. After the ceremony, the combatants were viewed as superior to their uninitiated peers because—as loathsome and crazy as war was—it was still thought to impart wisdom that nothing else could.

Following both world wars, Indian veterans turned to traditional ceremonies on their reservations to ease the transition to civilian life. The Kiowa Gourd Dance, in particular, was popularized across tribal boundaries in an attempt to heal the psychic wounds of war. During the 1980s, the Vietnam Era Veterans Inter-Tribal Association began holding a yearly summer powwow in Oklahoma that was open to veterans of all races. When they performed the Gourd Dance, captured Vietcong flags were dragged behind them in the same dirt their predecessors had dragged American flags in during the Indian Wars. "Warriors had to be recognized and were charged with the responsibility to take care of others, to practice self-discipline, and to provide leadership," one anthropologist observed about these ceremonies. "The social contract was assumed now as *wichasha yatapika* ('man' plus 'they praise')."

Contemporary America is a secular society that obviously can't just borrow from Indian culture to heal its own psychic wounds. But the spirit of community healing and connection that forms the basis of these ceremonies is one that a modern society might draw on. In all cultures, ceremonies are designed to communicate the experience of one group of people to the wider community. When people bury loved ones, when they wed, when they graduate from college, the respective ceremonies communicate something essential to the people who are watching. The Gourd Dance allowed warriors to recount and act out their battlefield exploits to the people they were protecting. If contemporary America doesn't develop ways to publicly confront the emotional consequences of war, those consequences will continue to burn a hole through the vets themselves.

I once took part in a panel discussion about war with the author Karl Marlantes. Karl is a good friend of mine, and I know that he draws an enormous amount of pride from having led a Marine platoon through some of the heaviest combat of the Vietnam War. At one point a very agitated man stood up and started screaming that he was a Vietnam vet as well, and that Karl and I didn't understand the first thing about war—it was all obscene, down to its smallest detail. Then he stormed out.

"That," Karl finally said into the stunned silence, "is one of the things that's going to happen if you truly let vets speak their mind about the war."

It's entirely possible that that gentleman saw little or no combat and simply harbors strong feelings about war. Or he might have done three tours in the heaviest combat there was and remains enormously affected by it. Either way, he is clearly in need of some way to vent his feelings to the wider community. Modern society rarely gives veterans—gives anyone—opportunities to do that. Fortunately, freedom of speech means that, among other things, veterans are entitled to stand on street corners with bullhorns and "disturb the peace." More dignified might be to offer veterans all over the country the use of their town hall every Veterans Day to speak freely about their experience at war. Some will say that war was the best thing that ever happened to them. Others will be so angry that what they say will barely make sense. Still others will be crying so hard that they won't be able to speak at all. But a community ceremony like that would finally return the experience of war to our entire nation, rather than just leaving it to the people who fought. The bland phrase, "I support the troops," would then mean showing up at the town hall once a year to hear these people out.

On Veterans Day 2015, the town hall in Marblehead, Massachusetts, was opened up to just such an event. Several hundred people filed into the hall and listened for more than two hours as veteran after veteran stepped forward to unburden themselves of the war. One of the first to speak was a Korean War vet who had tried to join the Marines at age fifteen. They turned him down but took his three friends, who were all killed in combat and buried next to each other on Okinawa. A couple of years later he paid his respects at their gravesites on his way over to Korea. An older woman stood up and said that she'd fought in Vietnam as a man and then had come back and had a sex change. Another Vietnam vet simply read quote after quote from Bush administration officials who—in his opinion—had lied about the Iraq War. My friend Brendan O'Byrne talked about meeting the mother of his friend Juan Restrepo, who had been killed two months into their deployment to Afghanistan. Restrepo's mother asked Brendan if he'd forgiven her son's killer, and he said that no, he hadn't. She told him he had to.

"That's when I began to heal," Brendan told the room. "When I let go of the anger inside me."

Today's veterans often come home to find that, although they're willing to die for their country, they're not sure how to live for it. It's hard to know how to live for a country that regularly tears itself apart along every possible ethnic and demographic boundary. The income gap between rich and poor continues to widen, many people live in racially segregated communities, the elderly are mostly sequestered from public life, and rampage shootings happen so regularly that they only remain in the news cycle for a day or two. To make matters worse, politicians occasionally accuse rivals of *deliberately* trying to harm their own country—a charge so destructive to group unity that most past societies would probably have just punished it as a form of treason. It's complete madness, and the veterans know this. In combat, soldiers all but ignore differences of race, religion, and politics within their platoon. It's no wonder many of them get so depressed when they come home.

I know what coming back to America from a war zone is like because I've done it so many times. First there is a kind of shock at the level of comfort and affluence that we enjoy, but that is followed by the dismal realization that we live in a society that is basically at war with itself. People speak with incredible contempt about—depending on their views— the rich, the poor, the educated, the foreign-born, the president, or the entire US government. It's a level of contempt that is usually reserved for enemies in wartime, except that now it's applied to our fellow citizens. Unlike criticism, contempt is particularly toxic because it assumes a moral superiority in the speaker. Contempt is often directed at people who have been excluded from a group or declared unworthy of its benefits. Contempt is often used by governments to provide rhetorical cover for torture or abuse. Contempt is one of four behaviors that, statistically, can predict divorce in married couples. People who speak with contempt for one another will probably not remain united for long.

The most alarming rhetoric comes out of the dispute between liberals and conservatives, and it's a dangerous waste of time because they're both right. The perennial conservative concern about high taxes supporting a nonworking "underclass" has entirely legitimate roots in our evolutionary past and shouldn't be dismissed out of hand. Early hominids lived a precarious existence where freeloaders were a direct threat to survival, and so they developed an exceedingly acute sense of whether they were being taken advantage of by members of their own group. But by the same token, one of the hallmarks of early human society was the emergence of a culture of compassion that cared for the ill, the elderly, the wounded, and the unlucky. In today's terms, that is a common liberal concern that also has to be taken into account. Those two driving forces have coexisted for hundreds of thousands of years in human society and have been duly codified in this country as a two-party political system. The eternal argument over so-called entitlement programs—and, more broadly, over liberal and conservative thought—will never be resolved because each side represents an ancient and absolutely essential component of our evolutionary past.

So how do you unify a secure, wealthy country that has sunk into a zero-sum political game with itself? How do you make veterans feel that they are returning to a cohesive society that was worth fighting for in the first place? I put that question to Rachel Yehuda of Mount Sinai Hospital in New York City. Yehuda has seen, up close, the effect of such antisocial divisions on traumatized vets. "If you want to make a society work, then you don't keep underscoring the places where you're different—you underscore your shared humanity," she told me. "I'm appalled by how much people focus on differences. Why are you focusing on how different you are from one another, and not on the things that unite us?"

The United States is so powerful that the only country capable of destroying her might be the

United States herself, which means that the ultimate terrorist strategy would be to just leave the country alone. That way, America's ugliest partisan tendencies could emerge unimpeded by the unifying effects of war. The ultimate betrayal of tribe isn't acting competitively—that should be encouraged—but predicating your power on the excommunication of others from the group. That is exactly what politicians of both parties try to do when they spew venomous rhetoric about their rivals. That is exactly what media figures do when they go beyond criticism of their fellow citizens and openly revile them. Reviling people you share a combat outpost with is an incredibly stupid thing to do, and public figures who imagine their nation isn't, potentially, one huge combat outpost are deluding themselves.

In 2009, an American soldier named Bowe Bergdahl slipped through a gap in the concertina wire at his combat outpost in southern Afghanistan and walked off into the night. He was quickly captured by a Taliban patrol, and his absence triggered a massive search by the US military that put thousands of his fellow soldiers at risk. The level of betrayal felt by soldiers was so extreme that many called for Bergdahl to be tried for treason when he was repatriated five years later. Technically his crime was not treason, so the US military charged him with desertion of his post—a violation that still carries a maximum penalty of death.

The collective outrage at Sergeant Bergdahl was based on very limited knowledge but provides a perfect example of the kind of tribal ethos that every group—or country—deploys in order to remain unified and committed to itself. If anything, though, the outrage in the United States may not be broad enough. Bergdahl put a huge number of people at risk and may have caused the deaths of up to six soldiers. But in purely objective terms, he caused his country far less harm than the financial collapse of 2008, when bankers gambled trillions of dollars of taxpayer money on blatantly fraudulent mortgages. These crimes were committed while hundreds of thousands of Americans were fighting and dying in wars overseas. Almost 9 million people lost their jobs during the financial crisis, 5 million families lost their homes, and the unemployment rate doubled to around 10 percent.

For nearly a century, the national suicide rate has almost exactly mirrored the unemployment rate, and after the financial collapse, America's suicide rate increased by nearly 5 percent. In an article published in 2012 in *The Lancet*, epidemiologists who study suicide estimated that the recession cost almost 5,000 additional American lives during the first two years—disproportionately among middle-aged white men. That is close to the nation's losses in the Iraq and Afghan wars combined. If Sergeant Bergdahl betrayed his country—and that's not a hard case to make—surely the bankers and traders who caused the financial collapse did as well. And yet they didn't provoke nearly the kind of outcry that Bergdahl did. Not a single high-level CEO has even been charged in connection with the financial collapse, much less been convicted and sent to prison, and most of them went on to receive huge year-end bonuses. Joseph Cassano of AIG Financial Products—known as "Mr. Credit-Default Swap"—led a unit that required a $99 billion bailout while simultaneously distributing $1.5 billion in year-end bonuses to his employees—including $34 million to himself. Robert Rubin of Citibank received a $10 million bonus in 2008 while serving on the board of directors of a company that required $63 billion in federal funds to keep from failing. Lower down the pay scale, more than 5,000 Wall Street traders received bonuses of $1 million or more despite working for nine of the financial firms that received the most bailout money from the US goverment.

Neither political party has broadly and unequivocally denounced these men for their betrayal of the American people, and yet they are quick to heap scorn on Sergeant Bergdahl. In a country that applies its standard of loyalty in such an arbitrary way, it would seem difficult for others to develop any kind of tribal ethos. Fortunately, that's not the case. Acting in a tribal way simply means being willing to make a substantive sacrifice for your community— be that your neighborhood, your workplace, or your entire country. Obviously, you don't need to be a Navy SEAL in order to do that.

In late 2015, while finishing this book, I saw a family notice in the *New York Times* for a man named Martin H. Bauman, who died peacefully at age eighty-five. The notice explained that Mr. Bauman had joined the army in the 1950s, contracted polio while in the service, graduated college under the GI Bill, and eventually started a successful job placement firm in New York City. The firm found people for top executive positions around the country, but that didn't protect it from economic downturns, and in the 1990s, Bauman's company experienced its first money-losing year in three decades.

According to the *Times* notice, Mr. Bauman called his employees into a meeting and asked them to accept a 10 percent reduction in salary so that he wouldn't have to fire anyone. They all agreed. Then he quietly decided to give up his personal salary until his company was back on safe ground. The only reason his staff found out was because the company bookkeeper told them.

Bauman obviously felt that true leadership—the kind that lives depend on—may require powerful people to put themselves last, and that he was one of those people. I contacted the office manager, Deanna Scharf, and asked her what Mr. Bauman had thought about the behavior of Wall Street executives during the financial collapse of 2008. "Oh, he was very angry," she said. "He was a lifelong Republican, he was a poor kid from the Bronx who made some money, but he was furious with what happened. He didn't understand the greed. He didn't understand if you have a hundred million dollars, why do you need another million?"

Bauman voluntarily served his country, served his

employees, and served other handicapped people by establishing a scholarship fund in his name. He clearly understood that belonging to society requires sacrifice, and that sacrifice gives back way more than it costs. ("It was better when it was really bad," someone spray-painted on a wall about the loss of social solidarity in Bosnia after the war ended.) That sense of solidarity is at the core of what it means to be human and undoubtedly helped deliver us to this extraordinary moment in our history.

It may also be the only thing that allows us to survive it.

POSTSCRIPT

—

WHILE I WAS RESEARCHING THIS BOOK, I READ AN illuminating work by the anthropologist Christopher Boehm called *Moral Origins*. On page 219, he cites another anthropologist, Eleanor Leacock, who had spent a lot of time with the Cree Indians of northern Canada. Leacock relates a story about how she went on a hunting trip with a Cree named Thomas. Deep in the bush they encountered two men, strangers, who had run out of food and were extremely hungry. Thomas gave them all his flour and lard, despite the fact that he would have to cut his own trip short as a result. Leacock probed Thomas as to why he did this, and he finally lost patience with her.

"Suppose, now, not to give them flour, lard," he explained. "Just dead inside."

There, finally, was my answer for why the homeless guy outside Gillette gave me his lunch thirty years ago: *just dead inside*. It was the one thing that, poor as he was, he absolutely refused to be.

ACKNOWLEDGMENTS

First and foremost I would like to thank my good friends and family who shared their thoughts and conversations about this topic and read various drafts of this book. Those people include Rob Leaver, Melik Keylan, Austin Dacey, Daniela Petrova, Alan Huffman, Josh Waitzkin, Brendan O'Byrne, and my mother, Ellen. In addition, psychologist Hector Garcia offered me incredibly valuable advice about some of the scientific aspects of this book. And Barbara Hammond provided a continual source of encouragement, wisdom, and advice that saved me from many blunders and dead ends.

I am also indebted to my agent, Stuart Krichevsky; my editor, Sean Desmond; and my publicists, Cathy Saypol and Brian McLendon. I would also like to thank Deb Futter and Jamie Raab at Grand Central, as well as Paul Samuelson, who handled the day-to-day details of the publicity effort. Mari Okuda also did another amazing job as senior production editor on the manuscript, and I am very grateful to her for her great skill with the English language. The book appeared in early form in *Vanity Fair* magazine, and I am grateful to Graydon Carter and Doug Stumpf for trusting my instincts on this topic. I would have been completely lost without the heroic efforts of my researcher, Rachael Hip-Flores, who managed to track down every bizarre and arcane request that I threw at her.

My father passed away in 2012. Many of the ideas in this book were formed during a lifetime of conversations with him about the complicated blessings of "civilization." The opposing point of view was brought into focus by my friend and surrogate uncle, Ellis Settle, who pointed out that white captives of the American Indians often did not want to be repatriated to colonial society. That idea stayed in my mind for thirty years, until it reappeared as a possible explanation for why so many soldiers that I knew missed the war they'd fought in. The two impulses seemed roughly analogous, and I decided to pursue that idea as far as I could. This book is the result.

SOURCE NOTES

The Men and the Dogs

Association of Certified Fraud Examiners. "ACFE Report Estimates Organizations Worldwide Lose 5 Percent of Revenues to Fraud." http://www.acfe .com/press-release.aspx?id=4294973129.

Axtell, James. *The European and the Indian: Essays in the Ethnohistory of Colonial North America*. New York: Oxford University Press, 1981.

———. *White Indians of Colonial America*. Fairfield, WA: Ye Galleon Press, 1979.

Battin, Margaret Pabst, ed. *The Ethics of Suicide: Historical Sources*. New York: Oxford University Press, 2015.

Beasley, Mark S., et al. *Fraudulent Financial Reporting, 1998–2007*. Committee of Sponsoring Organizations

of the Treadway Commission. http://www.coso
.org/documents/COSOFRAUDSTUDY2010.pdf.

Bennett, John T. "Lawmakers Push Defense Fraud, Waste
Report to Influence Supercommittee Cuts." *The Hill*,
October 23, 2011. http://thehill.com/news-by-subject
/defense-homeland-security/189247-lawmakers
-push-report-highlighting-11t-in-defense-spend
ing-waste-fraud.

Board of Governors of the Federal Reserve System.
"Why Did the Federal Reserve Lend to Banks and
Other Financial Institutions During the Financial
Crisis?" http://www.federalreserve.gov/faqs/why
-did-the-Federal-Reserve-lend-to-banks-and
-other-financial-institutions-during-the-financial
-crisis.htm.

Boehm, Christopher. *Moral Origins: The Evolution
of Virtue, Altruism, and Shame*. New York: Basic
Books, 2012.

Bowles, Samuel, and Herbert Gintis. *A Cooperative
Species: Human Reciprocity and Its Evolution*.
Princeton, NJ: Princeton University Press, 2011.

Boyle, Douglas M., Brian W. Carpenter, and Dana
Hermanson. "CEOs, CFOs, and Accounting Fraud."
Kennesaw State University Digital Commons@
Kennesaw State University, Faculty Publications,

January 2012. http://digitalcommons.kennesaw
.edu/cgi/viewcontent.cgi?article=3752&context=
facpubs.

Bryan, Wm. S., and Robert Rose. *A History of the
Pioneer Families of Missouri*. St. Louis: Brand &
Co., 1876.

Calloway, Colin G.. "Neither White nor Red: White
Renegades on the American Frontier." *Western
Historical Quarterly*, January 1986.

Ceremony, John C. *Life Among the Apache*. Lincoln:
University of Nebraska Press, 1968.

Coalition Against Insurance Fraud. "By the Numbers:
Fraud Statistics." http://www.insurancefraud
.org/statistics.htm#.Vgr8wflViko.

Colden, Cadwallader. *The History of the Five Indian
Nations*. 1727. Reprint, Ithaca, NY: Cornell University Press, 1958.

Colla, J., et al. "Depression and Modernization: A
Cross-Cultural Study of Women." *Social Psychiatry and Psychiatric Epidemiology* 41, no. 4 (April
2006): 271–79.

Commission on Wartime Contracting in Iraq and
Afghanistan. Final Report to Congress, August 2011:
*Transforming Wartime Contracting: Controlling
Costs, Reducing Risks*. Chapter 3, "Inattention to

Contingency Contracting Leads to Massive Waste, Fraud, and Abuse." http://cybercemetery.unt .edu/archive/cwc/20110929214354/http://www .wartimecontracting.gov/docs/CWC_FinalReport -Ch3-lowres.pdf.

Committee of Sponsoring Organizations of the Treadway Commission. "Financial Fraud at U.S. Public Companies Often Results in Bankruptcy or Failure, with Immediate Losses for Shareholders and Penalties for Executives." News Release, May 20, 2010. http://www.coso.org/documents/COSOReleaseon FraudulentReporting2010PDF_001.pdf.

"The Cost of the Wall Street–Caused Economic Collapse and the Ongoing Economic Crisis Is More Than $12.8 Trillion." *Better Markets*, September 15, 2012. https://www.bettermarkets.com/sites/ default/files/Cost%20Of%20The%20Crisis_0 .pdf.

Federal Bureau of Investigation. "Financial Crimes Report to the Public, Fiscal Year 2010–2011." https://www.fbi.gov/stats-services/publications/ financial-crimes-report-2010-2011.

———. "Insurance Fraud." https://www.fbi.gov/ stats-services/publications/insurance-fraud.

Federal Reserve Bank of St. Louis. "Overpayments Due to Fraud by Category." https://research .stlouisfed.org/publications/es/12/ES_28_2012 -10-05_chart.pdf.

Fieldhouse, Andrew. "5 Years After the Great Recession, Our Economy Still Far from Recovered." *Huffington Post*, June 26, 2014. http://www.huff ingtonpost.com/andrew-fieldhouse/five-years -after-the-grea_b_5530597.html.

Fuller, David L., B. Ravikumar, and Yuzhe Zhang. "Unemployment Insurance Fraud." Federal Reserve Bank of St. Louis Economic Research. https://research.stlouisfed .org/publications/economic-synopses/2012/10/05/ unemployment-insurance-fraud/.

Government Accountability Office. *Financial Regulatory Reform: Financial Crisis Losses and the Potential Impacts of the Dodd-Frank Act*. Report to Congressional Staffers, January 2013. http:// www.gao.gov/assets/660/651322.pdf.

———. "Improper Payments: Inspector General Reporting of Agency Compliance Under the Improper Payments Elimination and Recovery Act." December 9, 2014. http://www.gao.gov/ assets/670/667332.pdf.

Hallowell, Irving. "American Indians, White and Black: The Phenomenon of Transculturation." *Current Anthropology* 4, no. 5 (December 1963).

Heard, J. Norman. *White into Red: Study of the Assimilation of White Persons Captured by Indians.* Metuchen, NJ: Scarecrow Press, 1973.

Hidaka, Brandon. "Depression as a Disease of Modernity." *Journal of Affective Disorders* 140 (2012): 205–14.

Hunter, John Dunn. *Memoirs of a Captivity Among the Indians of North America.* 1824. Reprint, New York: Schocken, 1973.

"Improper Payment Amounts. (FY 2004–2013)." *Payment Accuracy.* "https://paymentaccuracy.gov/tabular-view/improper_payments.

Insurance Information Institute. "Insurance Fraud." January 2016. http://www.iii.org/issue-update/insurance-fraud.

Kastrup, Marianne. "Cultural Aspects of Depression as a Diagnostic Entity: Historical Perspective." *Medicographia* 33, no. 2 (2011): 119–24.

Kirmayer, Laurence J., Robert Lemelson, and Mark Barad, eds. *Understanding Trauma: Integrating Biological, Clinical, and Cultural Perspectives.* New York: Cambridge University Press, 2007.

Krieger, Lawrence S. "What Makes Lawyers Happy." *George Washington Law Review* 83, no. 2 (2015): 554.

Lee, Richard B., and Irven DeVore, eds. *Man the Hunter*. Chicago: Aldine Publishing, 1968.

Lehmann, Herman. *Nine Years Among the Indians, 1870–1879: The Story of the Captivity and Life of a Texan Among the Indians*. Albuquerque: University of New Mexico Press, 1993.

London, Herbert. "The Fraud in Our Entitlement System." *American Spectator*, February 2, 2012. http://spectator.org/articles/36133/fraud-our -entitlement-system.

Luttrell, David, Tyler Atkinson, and Harvey Rosenblum. "Assessing the Costs and Consequences of the 2007–09 Financial Crisis and Its Aftermath." Federal Reserve Bank of Dallas, *Economic Letter* 8, no. 7 (September 2013). http://www.dallasfed .org/research/eclett/2013/el1307.cfm.

McFadden, Cynthia, and Almin Karamehmedovic. "Medicare Fraud Costs Taxpayers More Than $60 Billion Each Year." ABC News, March 17, 2010. http://abcnews.go.com/Nightline/medicare -fraud-costs-taxpayers-60-billion-year/story ?id=10126555.

"Male Chimpanzees Choose Their Allies Carefully."
Springer Select, December 3, 2012. https://www
.springer.com/about+springer/media/springer+s
elect?SGWID=0-11001-6-1397452-0.

Matthews, Merrill. "Government Programs Have
Become One Big Scammer Fraud Fest." *Forbes*,
January 13, 2014. http://www.forbes.com/sites/
merrillmatthews/2014/01/13/government-programs
-have-become-one-big-scammer-fraud-fest/.

Morelli, Gilda A., et al. "Cultural Variation in Infants'
Sleeping Arrangements: Questions of Independence." *Developmental Psychology* 28, no. 4, (1992):
604–13.

Muller, Martin N., and John C. Mitani. "Conflict and
Cooperation in Wild Chimpanzees." *Advances in
the Study of Behavior* 35 (2005): 275–331. http://
tuvalu.santafe.edu/~bowles/Dominance/Papers/
muller_mitani.pdf.

Owens, Judith A. "Sleep in Children: Cross-Cultural
Perspectives." *Sleep and Biological Rhythms* 2, no.
3 (October 2004): 165–73.

Paine, Thomas. *Common Sense* (1776).

Parkman, Francis. *The Conspiracy of Pontiac and the
Indian War After the Conquest of Canada*. Boston:
Little, Brown, 1899.

Pennisi, Elizabeth. "These Animals Stick Up for Social Justice." *Slate*, May 22, 2014. http://www.slate.com/blogs/wild_things/2014/05/22/animal_social_justice_equality_in_bonobos_chimps_monkeys_lions_baboons.html.

Porter, Eduardo. "Recession's True Cost Is Still Being Tallied." *New York Times*, January 21, 2014. http://www.nytimes.com/2014/01/22/business/economy/the-cost-of-the-financial-crisis-is-still-being-tallied.html?_r=0.

Riedl, Katrin, et al. "No Third-Party Punishment in Chimpanzees." *Proceedings of the National Academy of Sciences of the United States of America* 109, no. 37 (September 2011): 14824–29. http://www.ncbi.nlm.nih.gov/pmc/articles/PMC3443148/.

Safina, Carl. *Beyond Words: What Animals Think and Feel*. New York: Henry Holt, 2015.

Schnurer, Eric. "Just How Wrong Is Conventional Wisdom About Government Fraud?" *Atlantic*, August 15, 2013. http://www.theatlantic.com/politics/archive/2013/08/just-how-wrong-is-conventional-wisdom-about-government-fraud/278690/.

Seaver, James Everett. *A Narrative of the Life of Mrs. Mary Jemison*. New York: American Scenic & Historic Preservation Society, 1918.

Smith, Harriet J. *Parenting for Primates*. Cambridge, MA: Harvard University Press, 2005.

Smith, William. *Historical Account of Bouquet's Expedition Against the Ohio Indians in 1764*. 1765. Reprint, Carlisle, MA: Applewood Books, 2010.

"Table 1A—Criminal Convictions." http://www.sanders.senate.gov/imo/media/doc/102011-Combined_DOD_Fraud_Tables.pdf.

United States Department of Labor. "Unemployment Insurance (UI) Improper Payments." http://www.dol.gov/dol/maps/statelist.htm.

"Welfare Fraud." *Federal Safety Net*. http://federalsafetynet.com/welfare-fraud.html.

Zaki, Jamil, and Jason P. Mitchell. "Intuitive Prosociality." *Current Directions in Psychological Science* 22, no. 6 (December 2013): 466–70.

Zarembo, Alan. "As Disability Awards Grow, So Do Concerns with Veracity of PTSD Claims." *Los Angeles Times*, August 3, 2014.

———. "VA Overpaid $230 Million in Disability Claims." *Los Angeles Times*, July 14, 2014.

War Makes You an Animal

Beach, H. D., and R. A. Lucas. *Individual and Group Behavior in a Coal Mine Disaster*. Washington, DC:

National Academy of Sciences/National Research Council, 1960.

Becker, Selwyn W., and Alice H. Eagly. "The Heroism of Women and Men." *American Psychologist* 59, no. 3 (April 2004): 163–78.

Burnstein, Eugene, Christian Crandall, and Shinobu Kitayama. "Some Neo-Darwinian Rules for Altruism: Weighing Cues for Inclusive Fitness as a Function of the Biological Importance of the Decision." *Journal of Personality and Social Psychology* 67, no. 5 (1994): 773–89.

Costa, Paul Jr., Antonio Terracciano, and Robert R. McCrae. "Gender Differences in Personality Traits Across Cultures: Robust and Surprising Findings." *Journal of Personality and Social Psychology* 81, no. 2 (2001): 322–31.

Dunsworth, F. A. "Springhill Disaster (Psychological Findings in the Surviving Miners)." *Nova Scotia Medical Bulletin* 37 (1958): 111–14.

Field, Geoffrey. "Nights Underground in Darkest London: The Blitz, 1940–1941." *International Labor and Working-Class History* 62 (October 2002): 11–49.

Fritz, Charles. *Disasters and Mental Health: Therapeutic Principles Drawn from Disaster Studies.* Disaster Research Center, University of Delaware, 1996.

Haidt, Jonathan. "The New Synthesis in Moral Psychology." *Science* 316 (May 2007).

Harrison, Tom. *Living Through the Blitz*. London: Faber & Faber, 2010.

Hourani, L., et al. "A Population-Based Survey of Loss and Psychological Distress During War." *Social Sciences Medicine* 23, no. 3 (1986): 269–75.

Johnson, Ronald. "Attributes of Carnegie Medalists Performing Acts of Heroism and of the Recipients of These Acts." *Ethology and Sociobiology* 17 (1996): 355–62.

Jones, Jon, and Rémy Ourdan, eds. *Bosnia, 1992–1995*. Printed in Bosnia and Herzegovina, 2015.

Lay, Clarry, Marlen Allen, and April Kassirer. "The Responsive Bystander in Emergencies: Some Preliminary Data." *Canadian Psychologist* 15, no. 3 (July 1974): 220–27.

Levine, Joshua. *Forgotten Voices of the Blitz and the Battle for Britain*. London: Ebury Press, 2006.

Lyons, H. A. "Civil Violence: The Psychological Aspects." *Journal of Psychosomatic Research* 23 (1979): 373–93.

———. "Depressive Illness and Aggression in Belfast." *British Medical Journal* 1 (1972): 342–44.

Mestrovic, S., and B. Glassner. "A Durkheimian Hypothesis on Stress." *Social Sciences Medicine* 17, no. 18 (1983): 1315–27.

Oliver-Smith, Anthony, and Susanna M. Hoffman, eds. *The Angry Earth: Disaster in Anthropological Perspective*. New York: Routledge, 1999.

Terkel, Studs. *The Good War*. New York: Ballantine, 1985.

Von Dawans, Bernadette, et al. "The Social Dimension of Stress Reactivity: Acute Stress Increases Prosocial Behavior in Humans." *Psychological Science* 23, no. 6 (June 2012): 651–60.

Wrangham, Richard W., and Michael L. Wilson. "Collective Violence: Comparisons Between Youths and Chimpanzees." *Annals of the New York Academy of Sciences* 1036 (2004): 233–56.

Wrangham, Richard W., Michael L. Wilson, and Martin N. Miller. "Comparative Rates of Violence in Chimpanzees and Humans." *Primates* 47 (2006): 14–26.

In Bitter Safety I Awake

Ahern, J., and S. Galea. "Social Context and Depression After a Disaster: The Role of Income

Inequality." *Journal of Epidemiology and Community Health* 60, no. 9 (2006): 766–70.

American Psychiatric Association. "Posttraumatic Stress Disorder." 2013. http://www.dsm5.org/Documents/PTSD%20Fact%20Sheet.pdf.

Axelrod, S. R., et al. "Symptoms of Posttraumatic Stress Disorder and Borderline Personality Disorder in Veterans of Operation Desert Storm." *American Journal of Psychiatry* 162 (2005): 270–75.

Barglow, Peter. "We Can't Treat Soldiers' PTSD Without a Better Diagnosis." *Skeptical Inquirer* 36, no. 3 (May/June 2012). http://www.csicop.org/si/show/we_cant_treat_soldiers_ptsd_without_a_better_diagnosis/.

Betancourt, Theresa S., et al. "Past Horrors, Present Struggles: The Role of Stigma in the Association Between War Experiences and Psychosocial Adjustment Among Former Child Soldiers in Sierra Leone." *Social Science and Medicine* 70 (2010): 17–26.

———. "Post-traumatic Stress Symptoms Among Former Child Soldiers in Sierra Leone." *British Journal of Psychiatry* 203 (2013): 196–202.

Bilmes, Linda J. *The Financial Legacy of Iraq and Afghanistan: How Wartime Spending Decisions*

Will Constrain Future National Security Budgets. Faculty Research Working Paper Series, Harvard Kennedy School, March 2013.

Blosnich, J. R., et al. "Disparities in Adverse Childhood Experiences Among Individuals with a History of Military Service." *Journal of the American Medical Association Psychiatry* 71, no. 9 (2014): 1041–48.

Breslau, N., et al. "Vulnerability to Assaultive Violence: Further Specification of the Sex Difference in Post-traumatic Stress Disorder." *Psychological Medicine* 29 (1999): 813–21.

Bryan, Craig J., et al. "Suicide Attempts Before Joining the Military Increase Risk for Suicide Attempts and Severity of Suicidal Ideation Among Military Personnel and Veterans." *Comprehensive Psychiatry* 55, no. 3 (2013): 534–41. http://www.apa.org/news/press/releases/2014/08/military-suicide-attempts.pdf.

Buwalda, B., et al. "Long-Term Effects of Social Stress on Brain and Behavior: A Focus on Hippocampal Functioning." *Neuroscience and Biobehavioral Reviews* 29 (2005): 83–97.

Cantor, Chris. *Evolution and Posttraumatic Stress: Disorders of Vigilance and Defence.* London: Routledge, 2005.

Chappelle, Wayne, et al. "Suicide Among Soldiers: A Review of Psychosocial Risk and Protective Factors." *Psychiatry* 76, no. 2 (Summer 2013): 97–125. http://www.sciencedirect.com/science/article/pii/S0887618514000656.

Congressional Budget Office. *The Veterans Health Administration's Treatment of PTSD and Traumatic Brain Injury Among Recent Combat Veterans.* February 9, 2012. http://www.cbo.gov/sites/default/files/02-09-PTSD_0.pdf.

Crombach, A., and T. Elbert. "The Benefits of Aggressive Traits: A Study with Current and Former Street Children in Burundi." *Child Abuse and Neglect* 38, no. 6 (June 2014): 1041–50.

De Dreu, C. K. W., et al. "The Neuropeptide Oxytocin Regulates Parochial Altruism in Intergroup Conflict Among Humans." *Science* 328, no. 5984 (June 2010).

Finley, Erin P. "Empowering Veterans with PTSD in the Recovery Era: Advancing Dialogue and Integrating Services." *Annals of Anthropological Practice* 37, no. 2 (November 2013): 75–91.

Fischer, Hannah. *U.S. Military Casualty Statistics: Operation New Dawn, Operation Iraqi Freedom, and Operation Enduring Freedom.* Congressional Research Service, February 5, 2013.

http://journalistsresource.org/wp-content/uploads/2013/02/RS22452.pdf.

Friedman, Matthew J. "History of PTSD in Veterans: Civil War to DSM-5." US Department of Veterans Affairs. http://www.ptsd.va.gov/public/PTSD-overview/basics/history-of-ptsd-vets.asp.

Gal, Reuven. "Unit Morale: From a Theoretical Puzzle to an Empirical Illustration—An Israeli Example." *Journal of Applied Social Psychology* 16, no. 6 (1986): 549–64.

Gone, Joseph P., et al. "On the Wisdom of Considering Culture and Context in Psychopathology." In *Contemporary Directions in Psychopathology: Scientific Foundations of the DSM-V and ICD-11*, edited by Theodore Millon, Robert F. Krueger, and Erik Simonsen. New York: Guilford Press, 2010.

Gore, T. Allen. "Posttraumatic Stress Disorder Clinical Presentation." *Medscape*. http://emedicine.medscape.com/article/288154-clinical.

Green, B. L., et al. "Risk Factors for PTSD and Other Diagnoses in a General Sample of Vietnam Veterans." *American Journal of Psychiatry* 147 (June 1990): 729–33.

Hanwella, R., and V. de Silva. "Mental Health of Special Forces Personnel Deployed in Battle." *Social*

Psychiatry and Psychiatric Epidemiology 47 (2012): 1343–51.

Helmus, Todd C., and Russell W. Glenn. *Steeling the Mind: Combat Stress Reactions and Their Implications for Urban Warfare.* Santa Monica, CA: RAND Corporation, 2005.

Hirshon, J. M., et al. "Psychological and Readjustment Problems Associated with Emergency Evacuations of Peace Corps Volunteers." *Journal of Travel Medicine* 4, no. 3 (September 1997): 128–31.

Institute of Medicine of the National Academies. *Treatment for Posttraumatic Stress Disorder in Military and Veteran Populations: Initial Assessment.* Washington, DC: National Academies Press, 2012.

Jones, Franklin D., et al., eds. *War Psychiatry.* Army Medical Department Center and School, US Army Health Readiness Center of Excellence, 1995.

Kimhi, S. "Levels of Resilience: Associations Among Individual, Community, and National Resilience." *Journal of Health Psychology* 21, no. 2 (2016): 164–70.

Kimhi, S., and Y. Eshel. "Individual and Public Resilience and Coping with Long-Term Outcomes of War." *Journal of Applied Biobehavioral Research* 14 (2009): 70–89.

Kimhi, S., M. Goroshit, and Y. Eshel. "Demographic Variables as Antecedents of Israeli Community and National Resilience." *Journal of Community Psychology* 41, no. 5 (2013): 631–43.

Kinney, Wayne. "Comparing PTSD Among Returning War Veterans." *Journal of Military and Veterans' Health* 20, no. 3 (August 2013). http://jmvh.org/article/comparing-ptsd-among-returning-war-veterans/.

Kohrt, B. A., et al. "Comparison of Mental Health Between Former Child Soldiers and Children Never Conscripted by Armed Groups in Nepal." *Journal of the American Medical Association* 300, no. 6 (August 2008).

———. "Designing Mental Health Interventions Informed by Child Development and Human Biology Theory." *American Journal of Human Biology* 27 (2015): 27–40.

Lee, Michelle Ye Hee. "The Missing Context Behind the Widely Cited Statistic That There Are 22 Veteran Suicides a Day." *Washington Post*, February 4, 2015.

Levav, I., H. Greenfeld, and E. Baruch. "Psychiatric Combat Reactions During the Yom Kippur War." *American Journal of Psychiatry* 136, no. 5 (1979).

Litz, Brett T., and William E. Schlenger. "PTSD in Service Members and New Veterans of the Iraq and Afghanistan War: A Bibliography and Critique." *PTSD Research Quarterly* 20, no. 1 (Winter 2009). http://www.ptsd.va.gov/professional/newsletters/research-quarterly/V20N1.pdf.

McCall, George J., and Patricia A. Resick. "A Pilot Study of PTSD Symptoms Among Kalahari Bushmen." *Journal of Traumatic Stress* 16, no. 5 (October 2003).

McNally, Richard J., and Christopher B. Freuh. "Why Are Iraq and Afghanistan War Veterans Seeking PTSD Disability Compensation at Unprecedented Rates?" *Journal of Anxiety Disorders* 27 (2013): 520–26.

Marlowe, David H. *Cohesion, Anticipated Breakdown, and Endurance in Battle: Considerations for Severe and High Intensity Combat*. Unpublished manuscript, Washington, DC: Walter Reed Army Institute of Research, 1979.

————. *The Psychological and Psychosocial Consequences of Combat and Deployment with Special Emphasis on the Gulf War*. Santa Monica, CA: RAND Corporation, 2001.

Medical Surveillance Monthly Report 20, no. 3 (March

2013). https://www.afhsc.mil/documents/pubs/ msmrs/2013/v20_no3.pdf.

Morley, Christopher A., and Brandon A. Kohrt. "Impact of Peer Support on PTSD, Hope, and Functional Impairment." *Journal of Aggression, Maltreatment and Trauma* 22 (2013): 714–34.

National Center for Veterans Analysis and Statistics. "Trends in the Geographic Distribution of VA Expenditures (GDX): FY2000 to FY2009." http://www.va.gov/vetdata/docs/QuickFacts/ Expenditures_quickfacts.pdf.

Nock, Matthew K., et al. "Cross-National Analysis of the Associations Among Mental Disorders and Suicidal Behavior: Findings from the WHO World Mental Health Surveys." *PLoS Medicine* 6, no. 8 (2009); 6:e1000123.

———. "Suicide Among Soldiers: A Review of Psychosocial Risk and Protective Factors." *Psychiatry* 76, no. 2 (2013): 97–125. http://www.ncbi.nlm .nih.gov/pmc/articles/PMC4060831/.

Norris, F. H., et al. "Community Resilience as a Metaphor, Theory, Set of Capacities, and Strategy for Disaster Readiness." *American Journal of Community Psychology* 41, no. 1–2 (2008): 127–50.

Otto, Jean L., and Bryant J. Webber. "Mental Health Diagnoses and Counseling Among Pilots of Remotely Piloted Aircraft in the United States Air Force." *Medical Surveillance Monthly Report* 20, no. 3 (March 2013).

Philipps, Dave. "Study Finds No Link Between Military Suicide Rate and Deployments." *New York Times*, April 1, 2015.

Pietrzak, R. H., et al. "Psychosocial Buffers of Stress, Depressive Symptoms, and Psychosocial Difficulties in Veterans of Operation Enduring Freedom and Iraqi Freedom." *Journal of Affective Disorders* 120 (2010): 188–92.

Powers, M. B., et al. "A Meta-analytic Review of Prolonged Exposure for Posttraumatic Stress Disorder." *Clinical Psychology Review* 30 (2010): 635–41.

Shah, Sabir. "US Wars in Afghanistan, Iraq to Cost $6 Trillion." *Global Research News*, February 12, 2014. http://www.globalresearch.ca/us-wars-in-afghanistan-iraq -to-cost-6-trillion/5350789.

Tanielian, Terri, and Lisa H. Jaycox, eds. *Invisible Wounds of War: Psychological and Cognitive Injuries, Their Consequences, and Services to Assist Recovery*. Santa Monica, CA: RAND Corporation,

2008. http://www.rand.org/content/dam/rand/pubs/monographs/2008/RAND_MG720.sum.pdf.

Thompson, Mark. "They Don't Seem to Get Better..." *Time*, February 23, 2012. http://nation.time.com/2012/02/23/they-dont-seem-to-get-better/.

Toll, W. A., et al. "Promoting Mental Health and Psychosocial Well-Being in Children Affected by Political Violence." In *Handbook of Resilience in Children of War*, edited by Chandi Fernando and Michel Ferrari. New York: Springer, 2013.

Vedantam, Shankar. "VA Benefits System for PTSD Victims Is Criticized." *Washington Post*, May 9, 2007. http://www.washingtonpost.com/wp-dyn/content/article/2007/05/08/AR2007050801746.html.

"Veteran Statistics: PTSD, Depression, TBI, Suicide." *Veterans and PTSD*. http://www.veteransandptsd.com/PTSD-statistics.html.

Yehuda, R., et al. "Predicting the Development of Posttraumatic Stress Disorder from Acute Response to a Traumatic Event." *Biological Psychiatry* 44 (1998): 1305–13.

Zarembo, Alan. "As Disability Awards Grow, So Do Concerns with Veracity of PTSD Claims." *Los Angeles Times*, August 3, 2014.

————. "Detailed Study Confirms High Suicide Rate Among Recent Veterans." *Los Angeles Times*, January 14, 2015.

————. "A Misunderstood Statistic: 22 Military Veteran Suicides a Day." *Los Angeles Times*, December 20, 2013.

Calling Home from Mars

American Foundation for Suicide Prevention. "Facts and Figures." https://www.afsp.org/ understanding-suicide/facts-and-figures.

Andriotis, Annamaria, Laura Kusisto, and Joe Light. "After Foreclosures, Home Buyers Are Back." *Wall Street Journal*, April 8, 2015. http://www .wsj.com/articles/after-foreclosures-home-buyers -are-back-1428538655.

Apuzzo, Matt, and Ben Protess. "Justice Department Sets Sights on Wall Street Executives." *New York Times*, September 9, 2015. http://www.nytimes .com/2015/09/10/us/politics/new-justice-dept-rules -aimed-at-prosecuting-corporate-executives.html.

Breslow, Jason M. "Were Bankers Jailed in Past Financial Crises?" *Frontline*, January 22, 2013. http://www.pbs.org/wgbh/frontline/article/ were-bankers-jailed-in-past-financial-crises/.

Bureau of Labor Statistics. "Labor Force Statistics from the Current Population Survey." http://data.bls.gov/pdq/SurveyOutputServlet?request_action=wh&graph_name=LN_cpsbref3.

Centers for Disease Control and Prevention. "CDC Study Finds Suicide Rates Rise and Fall with Economy." April 14, 2011. http://www.cdc.gov/media/releases/2011/p0414_suiciderates.html.

CIA World Factbook. "Country Comparison: Population Below Poverty Line." https://www.cia.gov/library/publications/the-world-factbook/rankorder/2046rank.html.

Dvorak, Phred. "Poor Year Doesn't Stop CEO Bonuses." *Wall Street Journal*, March 18, 2009. http://www.wsj.com/articles/SB123698866439126029.

Eaglesham, Jean. "Missing: Stats on Crisis Convictions." *Wall Street Journal*, May 13, 2012. http://www.wsj.com/articles/SB10001424052702303505504577401911741048088.

Eisinger, Jesse. "Why Only One Top Banker Went to Jail for the Financial Crisis." *New York Times Magazine*, April 30, 2014. http://www.nytimes.com/2014/05/04/magazine/only-one-top-banker-jail-financial-crisis.html?_r=0.

Finklea, Kristin M. *Economic Downturns and Crime*. Congressional Research Service, December 19, 2011. https://www.fas.org/sgp/crs/misc/R40726.pdf.

Follman, Mark, et al. "US Mass Shootings, 1982–2015: Data from *Mother Jones*' Investigation." *Mother Jones*, December 28, 2012. http://www.motherjones.com/politics/2012/12/mass-shootings-mother-jones-full-data.

Gongloff, Mark. "Banks Repaid Fed Bailout with Other Fed Money: Government Report." *Huffington Post*, March 9, 2012. http://www.huffingtonpost.com/2012/03/09/bank-tarp_n_1335006.html.

Goodman, Christopher J., and Steven M. Mance. "Employment Loss and the 2007–9 Recession: An Overview." *Monthly Labor Review*, April 2011. http://www.bls.gov/mlr/2011/04/art1full.pdf.

Greenwald, Glenn. "The Real Story of How 'Untouchable' Wall Street Execs Avoided Prosecution." *Business Insider*, January 23, 2013. http://www.businessinsider.com/why-wall-street-execs-werent-prosecuted-2013-1.

Grinnell, G. B. "The Cheyenne Medicine Lodge." *American Anthropologist*, New Series, 16, no. 2 (1914): 245–56.

SOURCE NOTES

Holland, Joshua. "Hundreds of Wall Street Execs Went to Prison During the Last Fraud-Fueled Bank Crisis." *Moyers & Company*, September 17, 2013. http://billmoyers.com/2013/09/17/hundreds-of-wall-street-execs-went-to-prison-during-the-last-fraud-fueled-bank-crisis/.

"Home Foreclosure Rates Are Comparable to the Great Depression." *Washington's Blog*, May 7, 2013. http://www.washingtonsblog.com/2013/05/have-more-people-lost-their-homes-than-during-the-great-depression.html.

Kiel, Paul, and Dan Nguyen. "The State of the Bailout." *ProPublica*. https://projects.propublica.org/bailout/.

Leonhardt, David, and Kevin Quealy. "The American Middle Class Is No Longer the World's Richest." *The Upshot, New York Times*, April 22, 2014. http://www.nytimes.com/2014/04/23/upshot/the-american-middle-class-is-no-longer-the-worlds-richest.html?rref=upshot.

Llanos, Miguel. "Crime in Decline, but Why? Low Inflation Among Theories." *Crime & Courts*, NBC News, September 20, 2011. http://www.nbcnews.com/id/44578241/ns/us_news-crime

_and_courts/t/crime-decline-why-low-inflation -among-theories/#.VogoL_krLIU.

Newman, K. S., et al. *Rampage: The Social Roots of School Shootings*. New York: Basic Books, 2004.

"9 Wall Street Execs Who Cashed In on the Crisis." *Mother Jones*, January/February 2010. http://www.motherjones.com/politics/2010/01/ wall-street-bailout-executive-compensation.

O'Nell, T. D. "'Coming Home' Among Northern Plains Vietnam Veterans: Psychological Transformations in Pragmatic Perspective." *Ethos* 27, no. 4 (2000): 441–65.

Reeves, Aaron, Martin McKee, and David Stuckler. "Economic Suicides in the Great Recession in Europe and North America." *British Journal of Psychiatry* 205, no. 3 (September 2014): 246–47. http://bjp.rcpsych.org/content/205/3/246.

Savage, Charlie, and Andrew W. Lehren. "Can Bowe Bergdahl Be Tied to 6 Lost Lives? Facts Are Murky." *New York Times*, June 3, 2014. http:// www.nytimes.com/2014/06/04/world/middleeast/ can-gi-be-tied-to-6-lost-lives-facts-are-murky.html.

Story, Louise, and Eric Dash. "Bankers Reaped Lavish Bonuses During Bailouts." *New York Times*, July

30, 2009. http://www.nytimes.com/2009/07/31/
business/31pay.html.

Tapper, Jake. "How Did 6 Die After Bowe Bergdahl's
Disappearance?" CNN, June 9, 2014. http://www
.cnn.com/2014/06/08/us/bergdahl-search-soldiers/.

Thompson, Derek. "Why Did Crime Fall During
the Great Recession?" *Atlantic*, May 31, 2011.
http://www.theatlantic.com/business/archive/
2011/05/why-did-crime-fall-during-the-great
-recession/239696/.

Thompson, Mark. "The 6 U.S. Soldiers Who Died
Searching for Bowe Bergdahl." *Time*, June 2,
2014. http://time.com/2809352/bowe-bergdahl
-deserter-army-taliban/.

Uggen, Chris, and Suzy McElrath. "Six Social Sources
of the U.S. Crime Drop." *The Society Pages*, February 4, 2013. http://thesocietypages.org/papers/
crime-drop/.

"Unemployment and Job Insecurity Linked to
Increased Risk of Suicide." *PubMed Health*,
February 11, 2015. http://www.ncbi.nlm.nih
.gov/pubmedhealth/behindtheheadlines/news/
2015-02-11-unemployment-and-job-insecurity
-linked-to-increased-risk-of-suicide/.

United States Census Bureau. "Poverty: 2014 High-lights." https://www.census.gov/hhes/www/poverty/about/overview/.

"US & Allied Killed." *Costs of War*, Watson Institute, Brown University. http://watson.brown.edu/costsofwar/costs/human/military/killed.

Wilson, John P., and Catherine So-kum Tang, eds. *Cross-Cultural Assessment of Psychological Trauma and PTSD*. New York: Springer, 2010.

Worstall, Tim. "The True US Poverty Rate Is 4.5%, Not 14.5%." *Forbes*, March 15, 2015. http://www.forbes.com/sites/timworstall/2015/03/15/the-true-us-poverty-rate-is-4-5-not-14-5/2/.